Preaching Pity

Studies in Nineteenth-Century British Literature

Regina Hewitt
General Editor

Vol. 11

PETER LANG
New York • Washington, D.C./Baltimore • Boston
Bern • Frankfurt am Main • Berlin • Vienna • Paris

Mary Lenard

Preaching Pity

Dickens, Gaskell, and Sentimentalism in Victorian Culture

PETER LANG
New York • Washington, D.C./Baltimore • Boston
Bern • Frankfurt am Main • Berlin • Vienna • Paris

Library of Congress Cataloging-in-Publication Data

Lenard, Mary.
Preaching pity: Dickens, Gaskell, and sentimentalism
in Victorian culture / Mary Lenard.
p. cm. — (Studies in nineteenth-century British literature; vol. 11)
Includes bibliographical references (p.   ) and index.
1. English fiction—19th century—History and criticism. 2. Sentimentalism in
literature. 3. Gaskell, Elizabeth Cleghorn, 1810–1865—Political and social views.
4. Literature and society—Great Britain—History—19th century. 5. Charlotte
Elizabeth, 1790–1846—Political and social views. 6. Women and literature—
Great Britain—History—19th century. 7. Dickens, Charles, 1812–1870—Political
and social views. 8. Didactic fiction, English—History and criticism. 9. Great Britain—
History—Victoria, 1837–1901. 10. Social problems in literature. 11. Social
ethics in literature. 12. Sympathy in literature. I. Title. II. Series.
PR878.S45L46   823'.809353—dc21   97-32896
ISBN 0-8204-3903-7
ISSN 1071-0124

Die Deutsche Bibliothek-CIP-Einheitsaufnahme

Lenard, Mary:
Preaching pity: Dickens, Gaskell, and sentimentalism
in Victorian culture / Mary Lenard.
–New York; Washington, D.C./Baltimore; Boston;
Bern; Frankfurt am Main; Berlin; Vienna; Paris: Lang.
(Studies in nineteenth-century British literature; Vol. 11)
ISBN 0-8204-3903-7

Cover design by James F. Brisson

The paper in this book meets the guidelines for permanence and durability
of the Committee on Production Guidelines for Book Longevity
of the Council of Library Resources.

© 1999 Peter Lang Publishing, Inc., New York

All rights reserved.
Reprint or reproduction, even partially, in all forms such as microfilm,
xerography, microfiche, microcard, and offset strictly prohibited.

Printed in the United States of America

Dedication

I dedicate this book to the two strong women
who have formed my life, my late grandmother, Piroska Lenard,
and my mother, Sandra Lenard

Acknowledgments

After having worked through this project twice, first as a doctoral dissertation and then as a book, I owe more at this point than I can ever repay, but I would at least like to mention some of my debts and express my appreciation.

I acknowledge that I owe my two mentors, Carol MacKay and Susan Sage Heinzelman, more than I can express. Carol MacKay has always generously supported me, educationally, professionally, and emotionally, for most of my graduate career; she has walked me through many stages of professional development and has always encouraged me (to quote the United States Army) "to be all that I can be." And, as for Susan Sage Heinzelman, who fostered the initial, embryonic idea for the project, well, the bottom line is that this book would probably not exist if not for her. Beyond mentioning my appreciation of the emotional support and advice that she has given me at critical moments, what more can I say?

I would also like to thank my other committee members from the University of Texas at Austin for their advice and support during the dissertation phase of this study, especially Ann Cvetkovich who, while always respecting my ideas and intentions, raised many difficult, important questions that I otherwise would never have thought of.

I owe a great deal professionally to several colleagues who have read pieces of this book in its various phases. The members of my dissertation writing group, Greg Vanhoosier-Carey and Holly McSpadden, read many cryptic and dubious drafts of some of my chapters, sometimes reading the same, barely-revised material many weeks in a row while patiently trying to explain to me that what I was saying either didn't make sense or wasn't supported adequately. Another graduate school peer, Alice Batt, also listened to some of my ideas for what was then my dissertation and responded with helpful suggestions and constructive criticism. During my time teaching at Alma College, John Ottenhoff and Michael Selmon, both of Alma's English department, read chapters of the book during its final stages. Lynne Ludy also did me the honor of reading and critiquing the first chapter.

The staff at the Humanities Research Center at the University of Texas at Austin deserves mention for always being gracious and helpful to me during the time I spent researching there. In addition, Alma College provided some professional development funds to help make this project make it into book form.

Even more importantly, I thank the friends who have provided most of the emotional support that has made it possible for this project to go on: Laura Grossenbacher, my graduate school apartment-mate and still my friend; Kenneth Kidd, whose sense of humor keeps me sane; Alice Batt, a good Victorianist and listener; Claire Miller and Denise Sechelski, my own personal cheering-section; my colleagues Howard Lubert and Susan Kadlec, for their friendship during my two years on the Alma College faculty; and last but not least, my other friends in Alma, especially Lynne Ludy, Elizabeth Cook, and Chris Van Dyke.

Finally, it almost goes without saying that I owe innumerable debts to my family. To my great sadness, some of the family members who were the most precious to me, namely my father, Michael Lenard, my grandmother, Piroska Lenard, my grandfather, J. T. Rodgers, and my great-aunt, Marika Goncy, did not live to see this book published. However, I know that my remaining family members rejoice with me in finally seeing this project come to fruition. In particular, I am grateful to David Lenard, Andrew and Veronica Lenard, Tom and Beverly Rodgers, Agnes Lenard, Cathryn Rodgers, and Kay Rodgers Macmillan. Most of all, however, I would like to thank my mother, Sandra Lenard, for all her support, and her unfailing confidence in me during these past several years.

Table of Contents

Introduction 1

Chapter One: Critical Visions and Revisions:
   A Critical History of the Sentimental 11

   I. "The Most Exquisite Sensibility": The Eighteenth-Century
   Origins of Sentimentalism 11
   II. Sentimentalism and Literary Criticism 23
   III. Mixed Feelings: "Extraordinary" Women and
   Traditional Feminist Criticism of the Sentimental 32

Chapter Two: Preaching Pity: Women Writers and the
   Development of a Victorian Cultural Discourse
   of Social Reform 45

   I. The Death of the Moral Economy: Social Change
   and the Need for a New Cultural Discourse 48
   II. The "Two Nations" and the Women Writer 53
   III. "The Talent of Female Influence": The Power
   of Sentimental Morality 60

Chapter Three: "Mr. Popular Sentiment": Dickens and the
   Gender Politics of Sentimentalist Discourse 77

   I "My glance at the New Poor Law": Pathos and
   Parish Boys in *Oliver Twist* 83
   II. "Sentimental Philanthropist," "Humanity-Monger," and
   "Feminine" Genius: the Struggles of a
   Literary Cross-Dresser 93

Chapter Four: "I Know Nothing of Political Economy":
   Elizabeth Gaskell's Call to Sympathy 109

Conclusion 135

Bibliography 143

Index 155

Introduction

This project initially evolved from three points of departure: first, my longtime fascination with Charles Dickens, both as a novelist and as a public figure; second, my interest in the relationship between nineteenth-century fiction and social reform; and third, my rapidly evolving commitment to feminist criticism. In my 1991 master's thesis, "The Gospel of Amy: Biblical Teaching and Learning in *Little Dorrit*," I argued that Dickens was a novelist who was deeply engaged with the Bible, particularly with the New Testament, and that his engagement with these scriptural and religious mores strongly informed his treatment of the heroines in his fiction. My argument was limited, however, because I did not go beyond this conclusion to analyze the actual assumptions that both Dickens and his audience would have had in understanding such a heroine or speculate about the possible ramifications of my insights for feminist readings of Dickens.

I began to read criticism and theory about the Bible in literature, especially in Victorian literature, books about the status of the Bible in Victorian culture, and more criticism about Dickens and religion. This reading led me to an interest in the ways that women writers used religion to gain cultural authority, and I began to research women writers' anthologies of the lives of Biblical women. I was intrigued by the way that these women writers used the religious and biblical authority embedded in these biographies to "teach" lessons to their contemporaries; the didactic tone of these works and the cultural authority that this seemed to represent became more interesting to me than my original idea.[1]

After working on the biographical anthologies for a few months, though, I realized that narrowing down my work to this extent was, for the purposes of the dissertation at least, a dead end. For one thing, there was no way to pursue my original

---

[1] This was an extremely popular genre in the nineteenth century; many fairly well-known women writers put together these biblical biographies, including Charlotte Elizabeth Tonna, Harriet Beecher Stowe, and Anna Jameson.

interest in Dickens anywhere in the project. More importantly, it did not seem to include the historical and materialist concerns with literature as *cultural* work that were becoming increasingly important to me. I was, I began to realize, just as interested in the Victorian period's burning social issues of industrialism, poverty, social class divisions, and gender divisions, as I was in a consideration of nineteenth-century women and religious authority, but I couldn't figure out how to tie these different concerns together.

These seemingly diffuse interests did not crystallize for me until I read Jane Tompkins' "Sentimental Power: *Uncle Tom's Cabin* and the Politics of Literary History" in 1992. Although I have since realized that Tompkins' analysis of sentimentalism needs to be problematized, the first time I read her reading of Stowe in *Sensational Designs* it was a revelation because it showed me a way to put together my political/ materialist interests, my interest in religious authority in women's writing, and my concerns about the way that this writing has been handled by literary critics. I also realized that Tompkins had detailed in Stowe much of what I had already noted about Dickens: that his sentimentality, his constant "unimaginative" allusions to the Bible, were part of some larger design, a vision of the world in which literature could transform public opinion and thus create a more sympathetic and morally responsible society. I quickly perceived that what Louis Cazamian had called Dickens' sentimental "philosophy of Christmas" was part of a larger aesthetic and ideological system, closely related to what Tompkins labeled as sentimentalism in American culture.

Tompkins' argument that this value system was created by, and primarily associated with, nineteenth-century American women writers was also intriguing. Was the same true, I wondered, in nineteenth-century British culture? Who were the British versions of Harriet Beecher Stowe? Although I had already done quite a bit of research on the Victorian period at both the undergraduate and graduate levels, no names came to my mind, which probably says a lot about how unknown many of these women writers are.

I started out the process of discovery by looking through several secondary works on the Victorian period, most notably Catherine Gallagher's *The Industrial Reformation of English Fiction*. I created a list of several "obscure" women writers, which I then used as an initial reference point while working at the Humanities Research Center at the University of Texas. The Wolff collection, an eclectic assortment of materials by women authors, proved particularly helpful. The opening sections of Gallagher's book had contrasted an eighteenth-century writer of religious tracts, Hannah More, against an obscure nineteenth-century social reformer, Charlotte Elizabeth Tonna, in order to demonstrate the different conceptions of free will that were operating in nineteenth-century social reform literature. The extracts from Tonna in Gallagher's book caught my attention because their tone and their conventions sounded so much like Stowe's in *Uncle Tom's Cabin*, so Tonna's name was the first on my list. When I read Tonna's works, I knew that I had found my "British Stowe," and my research since then, which has covered all of the previous criticism on Tonna and touched on many other sentimentalist women authors, has confirmed Tonna's importance.[2]

Jane Tompkins argues that the sentimental social reform novel was one genre in which a woman could speak with a voice of power and authority, and Tonna certainly exemplifies this insight. I see Tonna as one of the originators of sentimentalist discourse— a woman who carved out a niche for herself as a social activist and author. In her *Personal Recollections*, Tonna stated that in her childhood, she was fascinated by imaginative literature, especially by Shakespeare, but later came to believe that fiction was sinful and frivolous. She constructed herself in the autobiography as a woman driven to writing through a desire to enact political change, and as a woman driven to politics through a strong sense of religious mission. Tonna therefore created a role for herself that

---

[2]Later on in my research I found out that there was actually a direct connection between Tonna and Stowe—that Stowe was an admirer of Tonna, and had even edited an American edition of her works.

at least partially exempted her from traditional norms of female behavior, and she continually justified this role in the her writings:

> I remember the sagacious shake of the head with which the present Bishop of Gloucester . . . . remarked . . . "Missy will one day be a great politician." He was so far right, that Missy has since encountered many rebukes for indulging a taste not considered lady-like, and for striving to rouse the mothers of her native land . . . . And does Missy repent? Far, far from it . . . . (*Personal Recollections* 43–44)

By inserting didactic, moralistic "sermons" into her works, Tonna took upon herself the mantle of God's authority and by doing so was able to transcend her own powerlessness as a woman unable to vote, but she also linked divine retribution with political action—the readers who heeded her incitements and calls for public inquisition into these evils, would, by implication, be doing God's work.

This formula was a powerful persuasive tool, but Tonna also had another weapon: her convincing use of pathos to induce audience emotional involvement. *Helen Fleetwood* contains numerous pathetic deathbed scenes, and each one is again used to evoke audience sympathy and drive home the lessons the novel has to teach. These two main sentimentalist conventions, as I argue in my book, dominated social reform discourse in the Victorian period.

This idea of women writers using their culturally assigned religious and emotional "powers" to enact social change through their writing was, and still is, an appealing one for me. For one thing, it has personal resonance because it reminds me of my childhood, when my family's constant involvement in United Methodist church activities showed me a world where, for the most part, women ran things.[3] More importantly, it is philosophically appealing because instead of dwelling on the victimization of women as it is revealed in nineteenth-century

---

[3] The Methodist church has a long history of active female involvement in church affairs; this history seems closely linked to a nineteenth-century Evangelical emphasis on a more emotional, "female" spirituality and social activism.

British literature or narrowing the field by focusing solely on a small canon of "extraordinary" women, my investigation of sentimentalist social reform discourse shows women like Tonna taking culturally determined roles and turning them into strengths.

At this point, I would like to explain my use of the word "discourse" to describe the phenomenon of sentimentality and social reform in Victorian culture. There are many alternate words that could have been used to characterize this phenomenon, such as "genre," "style," "rhetoric," "structure of feeling," or "mode." I have refrained from using "genre" or "style" because those words, which are strongly associated with traditional, formalist literary criticism, imply the very kind of classification and judgment of the literary versus the non-literary that I want to avoid in this study. "Rhetoric" does not have such negative associations, but to avoid confusion I have not used the term to describe the totality of sentimentalist discourse, because I already use it to label one of this discourse's two defining components: the preachy, directly rhetorical mode of address sentimentalist writers used towards their audience. I do use the Marxist term "structure of feeling" in the second chapter of this book when I characterize the shift in audience/reader attitudes towards social problems during the nineteenth-century. The term could possibly also be used to describe shifts in discursive practice, but again, to avoid confusion, I have used it only to refer to the shifts in the cultural mind-set of the nineteenth-century reading public instead of to the sentimentalist discourse that constructed and reflected these shifts.

In her 1995 book *Melodramatic Tactics,* Elaine Hadley uses the word "mode" instead of "discourse" in order to describe a distinct style of representation based on the conventions of nineteenth-century stage melodrama. Hadley argues that this mode "was manifest in texts and speeches but also . . . [in] physical gestures, political actions, and visual cues, such as clothing and other objects" (4). She claims that "mode" is a more appropriate term than "discourse" to use when describing such a phenomenon because she sees discourses more as institutions (such as law, religion, science, etc.) with "material impact on a culture and its people because they inform many of the places and practices that organize society" (9). Modes, according to Hadley, are "less extensive, less powerful, and less autonomous" but nevertheless "exerted an impact on the production of cultural meaning" (10). This argument is a provocative one. I believe, however, that "discourse" is a more appropriate designation than "mode" for two reasons. First, "discourse" does not have the same connotations of shallowness and insubstantiality. After all, the word "mode" is most commonly associated with the fashion industry, and the textual practices that I deal with in this book reflect and represent major ideological changes. Second, the subject matter of my book, unlike Hadley's, is exclusively textual; I am documenting cultural changes with textual evidence and analyzing the reception and impact of these changes with textual evidence. Since "discourse," according to most standard definitions, commonly refers to verbal expression, it seems a more suitable term to use when referring to written materials. Other scholars, as I have suggested with my mention of Hadley, have argued differently.

Obviously, this book owes a great deal to other studies that have addressed similar issues. I have already acknowledged my indebtedness to Jane Tompkins. I would like to mention the following other critical studies in particular: Nancy Armstrong's *Desire and Domestic Fiction* (1987), Suzanne Clark's *Sentimental Modernism* (1991), Joseph Kestner's *Protest and Reform* (1985), and Christine Krueger's *The Reader's Repentance* (1992). It will be apparent by the end of the first chapter of this book that my methodology, my approach to feminist scholarship, is indebted not only to Jane Tompkins, but also to both Armstrong and Clark: to Armstrong because her Foucauldian approach to power relations shows how eighteenth- and nineteenth-century women writers were powerful; to Clark because her historicization of literary judgment, like Tompkins', illustrates that the label of sentimentality impacted women writers during the modernist period. Since I discuss Tompkins, Clark, and Armstrong and their approaches to feminist criticism at length later, I will not do so further here.

Joseph Kestner's *Protest and Reform: The British Social Narrative By Women* is a book that thoroughly documents the prominence of women writers in nineteenth-century British social protest literature. Kestner's study presents a large array of works by women writers for consideration, loosely organized by the decade in which they were published. The book is therefore invaluable for research purposes, because of its extended discussions of these then-obscure writers and their works. Kestner tends to evade the issue of literary value, however, by focusing on the *historical* importance of these authors and works; in fact, he often seems to apologize for their lack of literary merit:

> There is a tradition involving women, important to the development of both literary and social history, that is part of the tradition of nineteenth-century female authorship without being its most distinguished part. This is not a reason, however, for it to remain indistinguishable. (15-16).

Another interesting thing about *Protest and Reform* is that it scrupulously avoids connecting its subject matter with sentimentality. Even though Kestner deals with some of the same women authors that I do, namely Tonna, Frances Trollope, and Elizabeth Gaskell, he seems to go out of his way to avoid even using any version of 'sentimental' in relation to these women authors and their works. He occasionally uses words like "overdrawn" and "excessive" (55, 58), but his only reference to sentimentality is in regard to Dickens—one of the few male authors mentioned in the book. Kestner quotes Fanny Mayne's comment in *Jane Rutherford* (1853-54) that the 'two nations' formula is "no longer true, although it is still re-echoed by the maudlin sentimentalist," and he then remarks that Mayne "may be thinking of Dickens in her comment about sentimentalists" (Kestner 178). Given the fact that all of the women social reform writers Kestner analyzes were trying to influence public opinion through their fiction, and therefore had a clear interest in arousing public sympathy, it is odd that Kestner fails to address the issue of sentimentality. As I argue in the first chapter of this book, the idea that intervention had to come from the heart, not the head, clearly derives from eighteenth-century moral philosophy and sentimentalist literature. Moreover, the feminization of sentimentalism that occurred in the nineteenth century, a trend that I document in the first and second chapters of this book, also helps to account for the *dominance* of women writers in the arena of social reform writing—a dominance that Kestner documents and celebrates, but does not adequately explain.

Christine Krueger's *The Reader's Repentance: Women Preachers, Women Writers, and Nineteenth-Century Social Discourse*, which "reconsiders the history of women's social writing in terms of a female preaching tradition," is the book to which my own work is probably the most similar (Krueger 5). For one thing, Krueger traces the development of social reform literature by nineteenth-century women writers by drawing a direct lines of descent from Hannah More, to Charlotte Elizabeth Tonna, and Elizabeth Gaskell—three authors whom I also discuss at length and for much the same reason (Krueger 15). Secondly, Krueger's desire to "[re configure] lines of influence to include neglected and ideologically unfashionable writers" has clear similarities to my own approach towards feminist criticism, since I also believe that feminists have had a tendency to ignore women writers who have not been thought "progressive" enough (Krueger 5-6). The most important similarity between my work and Krueger's, however, is the fact that the "preacher" rhetoric she analyzes, a rhetoric which includes the use of biblical allusion, religious authority, and moral didacticism by these women writers, is one of the two defining characteristics of what I have identified in this book as sentimentalist social reform discourse. This likeness in our work leads to some parallel reasoning, and even the use of some of the same quotations from the authors we have in common: More, Tonna, and Gaskell.

On the other hand, like Joseph Kestner, Krueger is notably silent on the issues of sentimentality and sentimentalism. Two scholars may, of course, simply have a difference of opinion on how they choose to characterize certain works. While I emphasize the way that Charlotte Elizabeth Tonna used the emotionalism and pathos associated with the sentimental, Krueger praises Tonna's "realistic, unsentimental picture of her subject matter" (126) and, in another passage, the "unsentimental detail" with which Tonna describes factory life (133). The main reason for this disjunction is not a trivial difference of opinion, nevertheless.

Krueger's comments make it clear that she thinks of the word "sentimental" only as a term used to denigrate and suppress female writers: for example, she claims that Lewis Hippolytus Tonna's biography of his wife "manages to mute her powerful voice by applying the conventions of sentimental biography" (146). As I will argue at greater length in the next chapter, Krueger is essentially correct when she associates the word "sentimental" with negative critical judgment because the evidence shows that the term became increasingly censorious in literary criticism during the nineteenth- and twentieth centuries. As an aesthetic and philosophical system, however, sentimentalism was clearly an essential part of the cultural work performed by the writers Krueger and I discuss. Therefore, rather than evade the issue of sentimentality or retain the censure associated with it, this book will reclaim sentimentality as a necessary, powerful, effective, and culturally dominant aspect of these writers and their works.[4] Writers like Tonna used sentimentality deliberately and skillfully because in their cultural environment, to paraphrase Oliver Stone's 1987 film *Wall Street*, sentimentality was good. Sentimentality *worked*. Sentimentality was a crucial aspect of how these social reformers accomplished their goals because their works made use of commonly-held cultural values: namely, the reading public's association of women with sympathy and compassion.

The process of writing this book has, of course, led to complexities of which I had never dreamed when I started. It has led me to question some of my initial hypotheses: for instance, I now realize that the dominance of sentimentalist social reform discourse may not have been the uniformly positive phenomenon that I originally thought it to be. My research on the reception history of Elizabeth Gaskell, for example, indicates that the association of women with the emotionalism and moral didacticism of sentimentalist discourse certainly contributed to the problematic critical reception of women writers and to their

---

[4]By "these writers," I mean not only the nineteenth-century women writers that Krueger and I have in common (Tonna and Gaskell), but all of the writers I will identify as sentimentalist social reform writers in this book.

eventual near-exile from the literary canon. Moreover, sentimentalist writers' attempts to personalize and humanize oppressed groups through the use of emotionalism in the written word may have, perversely, gradually furthered the process of alienation that they had intended to reverse.

Two ideas are still clear to me, however. First, feminized, sentimentalist social reform discourse in nineteenth-century British literature is culturally important and needs to be studied. Second, the realization that standards of literary merit are historically constructed has opened, and will continue to open, a great many doors for the study of previously unrecognized texts. I trust that this book is consistent with those ideas.

Chapter One

Critical Visions and Revisions: A Critical History of the Sentimental

This introductory chapter will first define and historicize such key terms as sentiment, sentimentality, sentimentalism, and then go on to analyze literary criticism's treatment of nineteenth-century sentimentalist social reform discourse. Finally, I will address the feminist response to sentimentalism which, I believe, has been hindered by a distrust of the conventionally "feminine" nature of sentimentalist discourse, and by an imperative to create a feminist canon of the "best" female writers. For entirely different reasons, both traditional and feminist scholars have in large part rejected the traditional religious and social values that characterize the sentimentalist tradition.

I. "The Most Exquisite Sensibility": The Eighteenth-Century Origins of Sentimentalism

Although this is essentially a study of the nineteenth-century, any discussion of sentimentalist social reform discourse must begin with the eighteenth-century, because the idea that social benevolence had to come from the heart rather than the head was, in many ways, a carry-over from the eighteenth-century "cult of sensibility." As a philosophical system, eighteenth-century sentimentalism derived from the Lockean assumption that the individual human experience (as opposed to direct divine guidance) is the source of all knowable knowledge and values—which meant that, "The role of the feelings, especially in the formation of moral judgments, was particularly emphasized" (Brissenden 24). This assumption led to the "Moral Sense" school of philosophy's notion that human beings are innately sympathetic, or at least, that under the right conditions, humans are "naturally" capable of benevolence.[1] Locke's student, the second Earl of Shaftesbury, also understood the world through looking at the human consciousness at work, but "differed from Locke in wishing to see the openness of sensibility welded to benevolence," and this desire continued in the work of those who followed him (Todd 25).

The moral philosophers' doctrine of humanity's essential goodness was probably articulated in its most popularized form by Adam Smith in his *Theory of Moral Sentiments*:

> How selfish soever man may be supposed, there are evidently some principles in his nature, which interest him in the fortune of others, and render their happiness necessary to him, though he derives nothing from it, except the pleasure of seeing it. Of this kind is pity or compassion, the emotion which we feel for the misery of others, when we either see it, or are made to conceive it in a very lively manner. That we often derive sorrow from the sorrow of others, is a matter of fact too obvious to require any instances to prove it; for this sentiment, like all the other original passions of human nature, is by no means confined to the virtuous and humane, though they may feel it with the most exquisite sensibility. The greatest ruffian, the most hardened violator of the laws of society, is not altogether without it. (Smith 47)

Although some, like Hannah More, may have been suspicious of the idea that we are good because it feels good to be good, rather than because of obedience to divine law, this optimistic idea that human beings are naturally benevolent was extremely popular in the eighteenth century.

Smith's work was therefore widely known among educated readers in both Britain and France, but it is only one example of a widespread movement in eighteenth-century thought—a movement not only in philosophy, but also in literature, in religious belief and practice, and in the culture at large. As R. F. Brissenden has argued,

> It is in this period that the humanitarian impulse is recognised and consciously fostered in western civilisation, although the word "humanitarian" itself does not enter the language until the early

---

[1]This school of philosophy included Shaftesbury, Francis Hutcheson, David Hume, and Adam Smith.

nineteenth century. And this impulse, and the recognition of it, is in the original sense of the word, "sentimental." (Brissenden 33)

The sentimental ideology of moral philosophy was popularized not only by Adam Smith; it also entered into all literary genres. This literature—drama, poetry, essays, but, most importantly, fiction—showed people how to conduct themselves in relation to other people, and how to respond properly to their experiences, in order to further a larger goal of creating a kinder, gentler society.[2] Adam Smith's suggestion that we can feel pity "when we either see it [the suffering of others], or are made to conceive it in a very lively manner" resulted in the popularity of works that portrayed suffering in order to teach people how to respond to it. Moreover, this movement in thought and text also seems to have encouraged humanitarianism in deed. "The eighteenth century," as Brissenden has suggested, "is an age of great philanthropists" (81–82).[3]

The new cultural emphasis on feeling over reason also influenced religious belief and practice in the eighteenth century: namely, the way that John Wesley's Methodist movement made use of "sentimental" emotionalism. Wesley wrote in his *Journal* in 1773:

> I casually took a volume of what is called *A Sentimental Journey through Italy and France*. Sentimental, what is that? It is not English; he might as well say Continental. It convays [sic] no determinate idea; yet one fool makes many. And this nonsensical word (who would believe it) is become a fashionable one. (qtd. in Erämetsä 22)

---

[2]This literature "school" contained poets like Edward Young, William Cowper, and Thomas Gray, and dramatists like Richard Cumberland and Elizabeth Inchbald. The fiction included works both about the man of feeling (Henry MacKenzie's *The Man of Feeling* and Laurence Sterne's *Sentimental Journey*) and the woman of feeling (Samuel Richardson's *Clarissa*, Charlotte Smith's *Emmeline*, and Mary Wollstonecraft's *Mary: A Fiction*).

[3]Brissenden names in particular General Oglethorpe, the founder of the colony of Georgia, Captain Coram, the founder of the Foundling Hospital, and John Howard, the prison reformer.

Wesley's distaste for the word "sentimental" is ironic, however, given that Wesley himself claimed that "Methodism was, above all things, a religion of the heart" (Thompson, *Making*, 365). Opposed to the rigid doctrine of predestination preached by traditional Calvinists, Wesley replaced it with his message of justification by grace through faith. Wesley taught that an individual was solely dependent on God's grace (and so could not earn his or her way to heaven with good works), but also that grace could be maintained through faith. This faith could manifest itself in service to the Church, in "a methodical discipline in every aspect of life," and in "the cultivation of one's own soul, in religious exercises, tract-reading, but—above all—in attempts to reproduce the emotional convulsions of conversion . . ." (Thompson, *Making* , 365). The conversion experience, in which a believer felt him or herself to be moved by God's love and forgiveness, was the highlight of Methodist piety. Wesley himself considered that in spite of own lifelong record of exacting, methodical piety, he was not a true Christian until he experienced an emotional conversion experience where he felt his heart "strangely warmed" at a Bible study meeting in Aldersgate.

Indeed, much of the Methodist movement's success was due to its attention to enthusiasm and sentimental emotional drama. Janet Todd has noted that Charles Wesley's Methodist hymns carry many of the same themes and speech patterns common to the sentimental literature of the period: "In such verse God becomes a friendly Shaftesburian, while Jesus acquires the kindly qualities of the Man of Feeling (Todd 50). In "Love Divine, All Loves Excelling," for example, Jesus is "all compassion, pure unbounded love" (*The Book of Hymns* #283). Wesley's hymns also emphasize feeling, not reason, as the means of perceiving both sin and grace: in "I Want a Principle Within" Wesley asks God to instill "a sensibility of sin" within him , and in "How Can a Sinner Know," the question "How can a sinner know/ His sins on earth forgiven?" is answered with: "What we have *felt* and seen/ With confidence we tell" (*The Book of Hymns* #279 and #114, emphasis added). Those who disapproved of the Methodist movement also noted its indebtedness to sentimentalism, which by 1815 had already begun to be intellectually discredited. For instance, in his scathing 1815 piece on Methodism, the Romantic essayist William Hazlitt explicitly linked Methodism with sentimentalism when he claimed that Methodism represented an easy and essentially insincere approach to religion:

> How comfortably this doctrine [Methodism] must sit on those who are loth to give up old habits of vice, or are just tasting the sweets of new ones; on the withered hag who looks back on a life of dissipation, or the young devotee who looks forward to a life of pleasure; . . . the maudling sentimentalist, the religious prostitute, the disinterested poet laureate, the humane war contractor, or the Society for the Suppression of Vice! (60)

Eighteenth-century Methodism's indebtedness to the cult of sensibility is also discussed at length by G. J. Barker-Benfield, who describes the relationship between sentimental themes in novels and poetry and Methodist hymns, dress codes, attitudes towards women, and political beliefs, especially in regard to the poor and oppressed.[4] These similarities help to explain why, in spite of his distrust of fiction, Wesley approved of a novel like Henry Brooke's *The Fool of Quality* (1765), which is an idealistic account of sentimental virtues. As Markman Ellis points out, "the sentimental novel's rhetoric of physiological display and its focus on benevolence echoes Methodist teaching" (133).

This religious manifestation of eighteenth-century sentimentalism carried on into nineteenth-century piety, both in the Methodist Church and in the Evangelical movement within the Anglican Church; it would prove to be particularly important to the nineteenth-century writers whom I discuss later in this book. Because sentimental ideas and attitudes were acceptable in religious practice long after they were devalued in literature, and because the Evangelical movement encouraged women to take an active role in charity and church affairs, the ideology and rhetoric of the Evangelical movement became an important aspect of nineteenth-century sentimentalist social reform discourse.[5]

---

[4]C.J. Barker-Benfield, *The Culture of Sensibility* (Chicago: The University of Chicago Press) pp. 266–286.

[5]Christine Krueger, for instance, argues for a direct link between the Methodist tradition of female preachers and the

With the eighteenth-century sentimentalist movement, especially in literature, came a large vocabulary of feeling—most importantly the words, "sentiment," "sentimental," and "sensibility"—all of which derive from two Latin words, the verb *sentire* and the noun *sensus*.[6] *Sentire* means, generally, to be aware, mostly in the physical sense, but can also refer to mental awareness, "to feel, perceive, observe, notice" (Lewis and Short 1672). Similarly, *sensus* can also refer to either physical or mental/emotional awareness (Lewis and Short 1670–71). Derived from Latin root words whose meanings were already ambiguous, words such as sentimentalism, sentimentality, and sensibility were sometimes used interchangeably, and their meanings shifted significantly, even from the middle of the eighteenth century to the end.[7]

The semantic development of the word "sentimental" is a case in point. It made one of its earliest documented appearances in a much-quoted 1749 letter from Lady Bradslaigh to the novelist Samuel Richardson:

> What, in your opinion, is the meaning of the word sentimental, so much in vogue among the polite. Everything clever and agreeable is comprehended in that word, but I am convinced a wrong interpretation is given, because it is impossible everything so clever and agreeable can be so common as this word. I am frequently astonished to hear such a one is a sentimental man; we were a sentimental party; I have been taking a sentimental walk.
> ... (qtd. in Erämetsä 22)

---

didactic rhetoric of nineteenth-century female social reform writers.

[6] Also "sense" (as in moral sense), "sentimentality," "sentimentalism," "sentimentalist," "sensible," "sensitive," and "man of sentiment" (Brissenden 13).

[7] According to the *OED*, "sensibility," in the eighteenth and early nineteenth century, meant : "Capacity for refined emotion; delicate sensitiveness of taste; also, readiness to feel compassion for suffering, and also to be moved by the pathetic in literature and art" (Vol. IX, 461). In their original, positive meanings, both sentimentality and sentimentalism also referred to "refined and elevated feeling" (*OED*, Vol. IX, 471).

The *Oxford English Dictionary* proposes that the word sentimental, during this earlier part of the eighteenth century, seems to have had a generally positive connotation (as Lady Bradslaigh's letter indicates): "Of persons, their dispositions and actions: characterized by sentiment. Originally in favorable sense: characterized by or exhibiting refined and elevated feeling" (*OED* Vol. IX, 471). One example, in fact, even indicates that the word, in some contexts, may have meant what "sensible" does today, indicating cleverness or intelligence, which is almost exactly the opposite of what it means now.[8]

By the close of the eighteenth century, however, the word "sentimental" had taken on a more pejorative meaning, referring to those "addicted to indulgence in superficial emotions; apt to be swayed by sentiment" (*OED*, Vol. IX, 471). Both Brissenden and Janet Todd theorize that sentimentalism's fortunes began to fall with the failure of the French Revolution because the moral philosophers' ideas had come to be associated mainly with French philosopher, Jean-Jacques Rousseau. Rousseau agreed with Shaftesbury that human beings were naturally good and benevolent, but also thought that "the apparent viciousness of people" was due to "the evils of social and political institutions" (Todd 28). In *Emile* (1762), Rousseau expressed this idea in the "Confession of the Savoyard Priest":

> There is in the depths of souls, then, an innate principle of justice and virtue according to which, in spite of our own maxims, we judge our actions and those of others as good or bad. It is to this principle that I give the name conscience . . . . If it [conscience] speaks to all hearts, then why are there so few of them who hear it? Well, this is because it speaks to us in nature's language, which everything has made us forget. (289-91)

Accordingly, Rousseau called for a rejection of the traditional social order and for the intellectual and emotional freedom that would enable benevolence to flourish. It was this politicization of

---

[8]The *OED* provides this extract from an 1752 Horace Walpole letter: "I am still sentimental enough to flatter myself that a man who could beg sixteen guineas, will not give them" (OED, Vol. IX, 471).

moral philosophy "that made it possible for anti-sentimentalists later to blame both sentiment and Rousseau for the evils of anarchy and revolutionary France" (Todd 28).

One of the best examples of this reaction against sentimentalism is found in the last issue of the Tory satirical review, the *Anti-Jacobin*. Almost the entire issue is devoted to a poem by George Canning condemning "Sweet Sensibility, who dwells enshrined/In the fine foldings of the feeling mind," but whose "fair votaries, prodigal of grief/ . . . hear, unmoved, . . . Of crimes that blot the age, the world with shame. . ." (Brissenden 62). The personification of Sensibility is feminized, and her "fair votaries" are also obviously female. The poem is accompanied by a large fold-out Gillray cartoon, entitled "The New Morality;—or—the promis'd installment of the high priest of the Theophilanthropes, with the homage of Leviathan and his suite," which depicts a revolutionary mob doing homage to their idols, Justice, Philanthropy, and Sensibility. All three of these are female figures: Justice is an old Medusa-like figure with drooping breasts who waves a dagger in her hand while she tramples the scales of justice; Philanthropy is a corpulent woman who greedily clutches the globe in her arms; and Sensibility is a younger woman who holds Rousseau's works in one hand and weeps over a dead bird while her foot rests on the decapitated head of Louis XVI.[9]

I suggest that this satire is a cruel, but predictable, reversal of the way that earlier sentimentalist thought had valorized women. Both Nancy Armstrong and Janet Todd have argued that sentimentalism gave women increasing moral importance (although little temporal power) in eighteenth-century English society, particularly after the Restoration. Todd demonstrates this point with an analysis of Addison and Steele's periodicals, where "sentimental virtues of benevolence and compassion gained ascendancy over the [masculine] courtly values of wit and

---

[9] R.F. Brissenden's *Virtue in Distress* and Claudia Johnson's *Equivocal Beings: Politics, Gender, and Sentimentality in the 1790's* contain descriptions of Gillray's cartoon and Canning's poem. Markman Ellis' *The Politics of Sensibility* (1996) also contains a detailed analysis, using the cartoon itself as an illustration.

sophistication" (Todd 19). Moreover, these superior virtues, particularly sensibility, were specifically gendered as female.[10] In a sense, therefore, the rejection of the sentimental also meant a turn against women, against the special, qualities of feeling and emotion associated with women, and against women's writing, particularly where it exhibited these qualities.

The success of the Romantic movement in British literature complicates this issue, since the male Romantic poets greatly valued the affective, sympathetic qualities that the sentimental culture had assigned to women. As Alan Richardson has noted, "It is not coincidental that [Nancy] Chodorow's definition of feminine empathy—experiencing another's needs or feelings as one's own—recalls both Keats' negative capability" and the notion of sympathy central to Shelley's *Defense of Poetry*" (14–15). However, I agree with Richardson's overall argument that the Romantic identification with feminine qualities did not necessarily translate into an appreciation for women or for women's writing. Instead, Romantic male writers sought to appropriate or absorb female qualities, often "figuratively cannibalizing their nearest female relatives in the process" (Richardson 21).

Other critics have suggested that the male Romantic poets were concerned about being perceived as effeminate or unmanly: for example, Barker-Benfield argues that William Godwin's works after about 1799 were extremely concerned with avoiding the appearance of effeminacy (153). Anne Mellor's *Romanticism and Gender* (1993) presents an even more interesting argument in relation to Keats and gender. Mellor identifies Keats as a writer who "complicates the issue of gender and ideology" for several reasons. He took on "feminine" roles in life by mothering his younger siblings and by nursing his dying brother Tom. Contemporaries portrayed him as sensitive and almost girlish in appearance. Finally, he "was also more subtly feminized by being

---

[10]Armstrong demonstrates a similar argument with a variety of texts: namely, Samuel Richardson's novels and various conduct books, but she extends her conclusions beyond the eighteenth century. I also will go on to develop this issue of the "gendered separation of powers" more in my second chapter.

a lower-class writer" (Mellor 171–173). Looking at the famous review in which John Gibson Lockhart, writing for *Blackwood's Edinburgh Magazine*, identifies Keats as part of a "Cockney" school of poetry, makes it clear that this designation had not only social class, but also gender implications. Lockhart's review contended that Keats, like many other would-be poets of the time, had no business writing poetry to begin with because he did not belong in the literary world. In the beginning of his review, Lockhart conceded the "just celebrity of Robert Burns and Miss [Joanna] Baillie," but went on to say that their fame "has had the melancholy effect of turning the heads of we know not how many farm-servants and unmarried ladies; our very footmen compose tragedies, and there is scarcely a superannuated governess in the island that does not leave a roll of lyrics behind her in her band-box" (519).[11] By implication, then, both lower-class men and all women, whether educated or uneducated, are in the same category—a category that renders them as inappropriate or incompetent authors of poetry. By the end of the review, Lockhart advised Keats that "it is a better and wiser thing to be a starving apothecary than a starved poet; so back to the shop, Mr. John" (524). He also argued that poetry should be kept out of the hands of "fanciful dreaming tea-drinkers" who "exert their faculties in laborious, affected descriptions of flowers seen in window-pots" (521). These insults apply to city-dwellers, both male and female, but they also imply that poetry should be limited to those who have a broad exposure to life outside the home, which would also largely exclude women. Lockhart's review was also contemptuous of Keats' lack of education:

> The old story of the moon in love with a shepherd, so prettily told by a Roman Classic, and so exquisitely enlarged and adorned by one of the most elegant of German poets, has been seized upon by Mr. John Keats, to be done with as might seem good unto the sickly fancy of one who never read a single line either of Ovid or of Wieland. (521)

---

[11]From Lockhart's point of view, the talents and successes of Robert Burns, a poor farmer's son who became a poet, and Joanna Baillie, a female poet and playwright, were unusual.

This lack of exposure to the classics and knowledge of languages other than English would, obviously, not only have applied to lower-class men like Keats, but also to women, since women did not have access to university education. Of course, a few women (such as George Eliot later in the nineteenth century) successfully acquired a mastery of these subjects, but they were the exceptions rather than the rule.

Earlier in *Romanticism and Gender*, Mellor lists Keats as one of the male Romantic writers who was the most hostile to the female "bluestocking" writers of that period. She does not make a cause-effect connection between what she calls his "ideological cross-dressing" and his hostility, but she does suggest that "Occupying the position of a woman in the poetic discourse of the early nineteenth-century was . . . a source of anxiety for Keats" (Mellor 179). My investigation of Dickens in relation to the same issue, which I discuss in a later chapter, also suggests the possibility of such a connection. In other words, it is possible that Keats' attitude towards the women writers was related to the way that he was lumped together with them by the hostile, educated male critics of the period.[12]

The literary criticism of the Romantic era also shows that certain literary critics were quite adverse to what they saw as sympathetic emotionalism in the Romantics' poetry, especially if it was thought to be inappropriate or excessive. George Croly's 1821 review of Shelley's *Adonais* (a pastoral elegy on the death of Keats), again in *Blackwood's Edinburgh Magazine*, explicitly relates

---

[12]Although I had not read *Romanticism and Gender* at the time when I was originally writing my chapter on Dickens, there are similarities between Mellor's treatment of Keats and my treatment of Dickens in the third chapter of this book. Specifically, we use the same term, cross-dressing, to describe the phenomenon of male writers working with the genres, conventions, and techniques readers and critics associated with female writers. However, Mellor's work on Keats is more concerned with literary production, while mine on Dickens is primarily concerned with literary reception.

the poem to the poems of sensibility of an earlier period, "the raptures and sorrows in verse, worthy of any 'person of quality'," which, he claims, were a joke to "the more rational part of the public" (696). The review ends with a parody of *Adonais*, the "Elegy on my Tom Cat," whose object is, obviously, to make fun of Shelley's "nonsensical" and "inflated" grieving for someone he barely knew (700). "Elegy on my Tom Cat" is also interesting because it shifts Shelley's elegiac point of view to make the poem seem more effeminate. Shelley's poem begins in the first person, but in the opening section, much of the grieving is displaced onto the female figure of Urania, Milton's muse, whom Shelley posits as the "melancholy Mother" of all poets (Shelley 393). So, rather than expressing "unmanly" grief for an "inappropriate" love object, *Adonais* expresses the still feminine, but more acceptable, grief of a mother for a dead child. Croly's parody, however, mourns his tom cat, a love-object that is, by definition, both sexualized and male, and this change links the speaker, a satirical version of Shelley, not only with excessive emotion but also with effeminacy:

> Weep for my Tomcat! all ye Tabbies weep,
> For he is gone at last! Not dead alone,
> In flowery beauty sleepeth he no sleep;
> Like that bewitching youth Endymion!
> My love is dead, alas as any stone,
> That by some violet-sided river
> Weepeth too fondly! (700)

The two reviews I have discussed here are admittedly a limited sample. They suggest, however, that even in the Romantic period, some critics in the literary world were already hostile to sentimentalism, especially when it was associated with male writers.[13] These critics tended to be educated and male, and strongly protective of literature as an elite enterprise.

---

[13]For other interesting discussions of Romanticism in relation to gender and sentimentality, see Marlon Ross' *The Contours of Desire: Romanticism and the Rise of Women's Poetry* (1989), Isobel Armstrong's "The Gush of the Feminine: How Can We Read

II. Sentimentalism and Literary Criticism

By the mid-nineteenth century, the status of the sentimental was mixed. On one hand, the association of women with sentimental religious values, with sympathy, and with tender, compassionate feelings was a good and positive thing, encouraged by the culture. As I will demonstrate in the next chapter, the growing physical separations between social classes made sentimentalist social values even more desirable, if not necessary. At the same time, these values were increasingly associated with women rather than men. This association, also often termed the "separate spheres" philosophy or "the domestic ideology," opened the doors for women to become involved in political and social issues, since women's greater access to these affective qualities made them ideal social reform writers.[14]

On the other hand, in the high culture, the literary culture, there was also suspicion of these same feminized qualities, shown by the increasingly derogatory nature of the word "sentimental." When in 1857 literary critic Fitzjames Stephen disparaged Dickens' novels in a serious literary review by calling them "melodramatic and sentimental stock-in-trade," he was clearly using "sentimental" as a term of abuse, not as a compliment ("Mr. Dickens as a Politician" 8). Similarly, Jane Welsh Carlyle admired George Eliot's first novel, *Scenes of Clerical Life* (1858), because it was "full of tenderness and pathos without sentimentality, of

---

Theresa Kelley's *Romantic Women Writers*, 1995), and Stuart Curran's "Romantic Poetry: The I Altered" (in Anne Mellor's *Romanticism and Feminism*, 1988). Curran's discussion is particularly valuable, since he advances the argument that women writers during the Romantic period, such as Joanna Baillie, Anna Barbauld, Jane Taylor (and many others), were "a crucial link between Enlightenment social satire and Victorian concerns with social- and self-improvement" (194).

[14]I will go on to develop this point further in my second and fourth chapters.

sense without dogmatism" (qtd. in Ashton 189). The novelist George Meredith connected the sentimental with women, when, bemoaning the lack of the Comic Spirit in English literature, he blamed this lack on the dominance of sentimentalists, among whom were some men and "very many cultivated women" (91).[15] Likewise, W.R. Greg's "The False Morality of Lady Novelists" condemned the "fantastic and flatulent morality" of "sentimental" women writers (158).

The nineteenth-century literary critics who attempted to address the differences between male and female novelists make the growing association of the sentimental with women even more evident. Most of these discussions, whether positive or negative, follow the "separate spheres" philosophy in assigning the sentimentalist virtues and faults to women writers. For instance, George Henry Lewes' 1852 *Westminster Review* article, "The Lady Novelists," stated that "the Masculine mind is characterized by the predominance of the intellect, and the Feminine by the predominance of the emotions" (131-2). Although Lewes qualified this statement as "purposely exaggerated . . . to serve as a sign-post," his assessments of woman novelists (both individually and as a group) follow along the lines laid out by his initial generalization (132). For instance, he stated that women writers "[succeed] better in finesse of detail, in pathos and sentiment, while men generally succeed better in the construction of plots and the delineation of character" (133). He warned, however, that female "Sentiment without Observation [leads] to rhetoric and long-drawn lachrymosity" (137). In such statements, Lewes revealed his basic distaste for women writers who turned sentiment into any kind of social rhetoric, since he hinted that women are, essentially, incapable of success at abstract,

---

[15]Meredith, George. *An Essay on Comedy and the Uses of the Comic Spirit* (1877). Meredith also wrote a unfinished play called "The Sentimentalists" which (among other things) includes a satirical scene in which a group of women swoon over the "exquisite pathos" of a lecture that celebrates "woman descending from her ideal to the gross reality of man" (Meredith, *Miscellaneous Prose*, 17).

philosophical and political discourse.[16] He used his assessments of two individual woman writers, Jane Austen and George Sand, to support this point. Sand he admired as "among the highest minds of literature," but he disapproved of her "philosophy" because he claimed that it must have been the "reflex of some man whose ideas she has adopted." In contrast, he greatly admired the pathos of her works as "utterances of a soul in pain" and as "transcripts of her experience" (136). Similarly, Lewes appreciated Jane Austen because "there is nothing of the doctrinaire in [her] . . . not a trace of woman's 'mission'" (135). In other words, it is clear that Lewes saw women writers as successful only when they stuck to doing what he thought they were capable of doing; they failed when they tried to "write as men write" because "to write as women is the real office they have to perform" (132).

Richard Holt Hutton's 1858 assessment of Dinah Mulock Craik, "Novels by the Authoress of *John Halifax*," enlarges on and clarifies Lewes' nebulous hints about the deficiencies of women novelists, and it does so without Lewes' self-conscious awareness that there were exceptions to his generalizations. Hutton argued that women writers "have not yet succeeded as poets" because "though they have finer spiritual sympathies than men, they have not the same power of concentrating their minds . . . . and hence, such poetry as they do usually write, is apt to be mere personal sentiment without any token of true imaginative power at all" (467). He presented this assertion in order to justify his claims that "feminine ability has found for itself a far more suitable sphere in novel-writing than in any other branch of literature" (466), but that this ability carried with it "special advantages and special disadvantages" (468). One of these disadvantages was, apparently, women writers' tendency to overdo their "finer spiritual sympathies" (467). Like Lewes, Hutton also clearly concluded that women should leave the moralizing and philosophizing to men, since he asserted that these qualities were

---

[16]Lewes' earlier review of Charlotte Brontë's *Shirley* (1849) contains comparable generalizations (*Edinburgh Review*, 1850).

contrary to women's "delicate powers of perception" (469).[17] Accordingly, he singled out what he called didactic fiction, "which presses all the resources of art into the service of some small item of penal discipline or rewarding justice" as "the lowest class" of fiction by women novelists (480). Even though Hutton was "primarily . . . a Christian apologist," which perhaps should have made him more sympathetic to the sentimentalist agenda, and his own writing was "directly polemical," he found such writing on the part of women distasteful (Gross 82). Since Hutton was, according to John Gross' *The Rise and Fall of the Man of Letters*, "a representative spokesman for educated, mid-Victorian critical opinion" his conclusions are particularly important for my purposes (83). Unlike Lewes, whose scandalous lifestyle and occasionally controversial opinions made him atypical, Hutton was truly representative of the educated literary critics of his time.

In the mid-nineteenth century, therefore, we find a critical discourse that, while sometimes professing to value the emotionalism and moral outspokenness of women writers, also maintained a distaste for those same qualities. The "art for art's sake" stance of the late nineteenth-century aesthetic movement further complicated the issue by advocating a more non-rhetorical, non-discursive role for literature and the other creative arts.

For Walter Pater in 1889, for example, literary art had to be judged primarily according to its beauty as exemplified in its more formal qualities:

> And further, all beauty is in the long run only *fineness* of truth, or what we call expression, the finer accommodation of speech to that vision within . . . . In literature, as in every other product of human skill, in the molding of a bell or a platter, for instance, wherever this sense asserts itself, wherever the producer so modifies his work as, over and above its primary use or intention, to make it pleasing (to himself, of course, in the first instance) there, 'fine' as opposed to merely serviceable art, exists. (*Appreciations* 10)

---

[17]Like Lewes, Hutton ranked Jane Austen's "completeness and harmony" above any other woman writer: "In many ways, the natural limitations of feminine power are admirably adapted to the standard of fiction held up as the true model of a feminine novelist in the last century [namely Jane Austen]" (472).

According to this model, then, any literature which has an openly rhetorical or "serviceable" function does not count as art unless it overcomes that functionalism by also maintaining a self-consciously artistic style. Pater did go on to suggest that great art can be further distinguished from good art by the extent to which it is "devoted to the increase of men's happiness, to the redemption of the oppressed, or the enlargement of our sympathies," but, clearly, in order for a work to be considered great, it must already be good (38). From Pater's aesthetic perspective, in other words, literary art had to be possessed of the "fine" qualities of beauty before any of its moral qualities can be considered. Moreover, Pater's fellow aesthete, Oscar Wilde, pushed this ideal to an even more extreme stance when he said in his Preface to *The Picture of Dorian Gray* (1891), "There is no such thing as a moral or an immoral book. Books are well written, or badly written. That is all" (Wilde 17). Unlike Pater, Wilde professed the desire to divorce art completely from any kind of social responsibility or purpose. Of course, Wilde's predilection for epigrammatical irony—not to mention his own use of sentimentality in his children's tales such as "The Happy Prince" and sentimentality combined with moral seriousness in "The Ballad of Reading Gaol" and *De Profundis*—mean that this earlier pronouncement in the Preface to *Dorian Gray* should be taken with a high degree of skepticism. Nevertheless, it is clear that Wilde's epigram is a baldly stated version of where aesthetic critical attitudes were at the end of the nineteenth-century.

By the end of the nineteenth century, then, sentimentalist social reform literature was already in trouble with the literary critics on two counts: firstly, its topicality and openly rhetorical nature did not conform to the more formalist, aesthetic definitions for art; secondly, the emotionalism that had been so moving to contemporary audiences was increasingly seen as exaggerated and misplaced. Wilde's statement that "one must have a heart of stone to read the death of Little Nell without laughing" exemplifies this aesthetic disdain for the sentimental (Ellman 469). Since aesthetic literary criticism divorced literature from its contextual and rhetorical qualities and therefore judged it according to whether or not it was "pleasing," it became all too easy to dismiss scenes that became not-so-pleasing when they lost their original contexts and were analyzed purely for their formal qualities.

In the twentieth century, literary criticism became increasingly formalist—this formalism reaching its height with the modernist movement in the critical movement known as New Criticism. Not surprisingly, it was during this period that the status of the sentimental probably reached its nadir. In their arguments for the value of the sentimental, therefore, feminist critics Jane Tompkins and Suzanne Clark link the rejection of the sentimental directly to the formalism of New Criticism:

> In modernist thinking, literature is by definition a form of discourse that has no designs upon the world. It does not attempt to change things, but merely to represent them, and it does so in a specifically literary language whose claim to value lies in its uniqueness. Consequently, works whose stated purpose is to influence the course of history, and which therefore employ a language that is not only not unique but common and accessible to everyone, do not qualify as works of art. Literary texts. . . that make continual and obvious appeals to the reader's emotions . . . epitomize the opposite of everything that good literature is supposed to be. (Tompkins 125)

Suzanne Clark echoes this line of reasoning when she asserts that "The term sentimental makes a short-hand for everything modernism would exclude, the other of its literary/ nonliterary dualism" (9). Since the seeds of this dualism come from uncertainty about the sentimental within nineteenth-century culture, Tompkins and Clark overstate the case when they name modernism as the root cause of sentimentalism's exclusion from the literary canon. However, they are correct in highlighting the role of modernist New Criticism because, as Tompkins argues, it was during that period that the institutionalization of literary studies resulted in the dominance of formalist ideas over more rhetorical and moralistic models. Before this institutionalization and popularization of formalist criticism, the dismissal of the sentimental had largely been confined to literary critics, leaving popular culture relatively unaffected. For example, George Ford has shown that the death scene of Little Nell in Dickens' *Old Curiosity Shop* , while it was distasteful to intellectuals like Oscar

Wilde, Meredith, and others, was still meaningful to the larger late-Victorian public. Ford describes a "Dickens Birthday Celebration in 1886 that included recitations of original poems about Little Nell and other pathetic characters in Dickens, like Jo in Bleak House" (*Dickens and His Readers*, 61–62). Since the era of New Criticism, however, the formalist idea of what makes a literary work "good" has become so ingrained that it made the rejection of sentimentality "a knee-jerk reaction without parallel in literary criticism" (Clark 11). For instance, a recent edition of a popular reference work on literary terms and literary theory has defined sentimentality as "for the most part a pejorative term to describe false or superficial emotion" (Cuddon 857). Moreover, this reaction, through New Critical teaching methods and the work of literary anthology editors, has affected popular perceptions of literature as well.

This is not to say that there were not dissenters from that rigidly formalist viewpoint. For example, in books like *Counter-Statement* (1931) and *A Rhetoric of Motives* (1950), rhetorical theorist Kenneth Burke argued that art has a rhetorical effect on cultural history, and that the literary critic must consider these effects and not narrow his study to "pure" art because there is no such thing as pure art. He did not address the gendered nature of this formalist exclusivism, however. In England, F.R. and Q.D. Leavis emphasized the formal qualities of the text like the New Critics and "redrew the map of English literature" accordingly, but were also concerned about the function of art in society (Eagleton 32). F.R. Leavis admired the openly political *Hard Times* the most of all Dickens' novels because of its "moral perception" which "works in alliance with a clear insight into the English social structure" (*Dickens the Novelist* 206). The Leavises' ambivalence about Dickens' open moralizing, his sentimentality, and his status as a popular writer, however, is shown by their initial exclusion of him from their canon. As Terry Eagleton has put it, "Dickens was first out and then in" (*Literary Theory* 33).

Overall, however, the formalist model was dominant, and it had two advantages that explain its dominance as a guiding model for a discipline hoping to establish its legitimacy: for one, close reading as an analytic technique was easier to teach on a large scale, because it required very little contextual knowledge from students (Tompkins 194). More importantly, however, formalist New Criticism helped to "establish literary language as a special mode of knowledge, so that criticism could compete on an equal basis with other disciplines, and particularly with the natural sciences, for institutional support" (Tompkins 194).

Even a quick glance through some representative texts associated with New Criticism confirms the latter insight. From T.S. Eliot's famous metaphor comparing poetic inspiration to a chemical reaction in his essay "Tradition and the Individual Talent," and the painstaking deductiveness of I.A. Richards, to the aggressively scientific objectivity of Roman Jakobson and Arthur Crowe Ransom, all show this attempt to "specialize" literary judgments by making them scientific. This "scientific" formalism, as Tompkins and Clark have argued, confirmed the rejection of the sentimental, leaving behind even Pater's attention to the moral qualities of art. Ransom, for example, commended T.S. Eliot for having divorced poetry from other social values: "One of the best things in his influence has been his habit of considering aesthetic effect as independent of religious effect, or moral, or political and social; as an end that is beyond and not coordinate with any of these" (138). Moreover, Ransom's own idea of criticism was even more "scientific" than Eliot's: in his call for what he terms an 'ontological' criticism he attempted to map and dissect literary form by presenting a graph of geometrical shapes labeled with abbreviations, such as "DM" for "determinate meaning," in order "to show the parts which meaning and meter play in the act of composition" (299).[18]

With their emphasis on complexity and subtlety, it is no wonder that critics of this period found the category of the sentimental to be a convenient insult. For example, I.A. Richard's project in *Practical Criticism* was not only to carefully analyze every aspect of the poetry itself, but also to carefully analyze

---

[18]Ransom later takes Eliot to task for having let his religious conversion influence him as a thinker: "Had Mr. Eliot only served his 'literature' with half the zeal he served his religion!" (207).

sentimentalist literature, which is openly rhetorical and didactic, encourages, in fact demands, a stock, conventional response from the reader, it goes against everything that Richards believed in. His remarks on the subject of sentimentality, therefore, are no surprise: "Among the politer terms of abuse there are few so effective as 'sentimental.' Not very long ago, the word "silly" was fairly useful for this purpose" (241). After dismissing sentimentality, Richards attempted to account for it by suggesting that it was caused by emotional and physical weakness:

> Certain rhythms . . . and sounds . . . all of these readily facilitate emotional orgies. So do certain conditions of mass suggestion. Reunions, processions; we often have to blush for our sentimentality when we escape from the crowd. Most remarkable of all, perhaps, are some effects of illness. I reluctantly recall that the last time I had influenza a very stupid novel filled my eyes with tears again and again until I could not see the pages. . . . [I]ndividuals vary amazingly. Some people regard indulgence in the soft and tender emotions as always creditable, and they wallow in them so greedily that one is forced to regard them as emotionally starved. (243)

In order to account for the sentimental, then, Richards constructed a pathology in which "indulgence in the soft and tender emotions" became either the effect of a physical illness or the sign of an emotional deficiency. This kind of critical attitude has so effectively dismissed sentimentalist texts that in spite of feminist and postmodernist efforts, the critical prejudice against the sentimental still remains basically intact.

Tompkins and Clark, as feminist critics studying American literature, have shown that this modernist dismissal of the sentimental effectually eradicated sentimental women writers, like Harriet Beecher Stowe, Susan Warner, and Fanny Fern, who dominated popular nineteenth-century American literature, from the American literary canon. My work with the reception of British sentimentalist social reform discourse leads me to make similar conclusions. In the succeeding chapters, I further address the literary reception of individual authors in order to show how the success of formalist/modernist literary criticism adversely affected the reputations of nineteenth-century writers who used the conventions of sentimentalist discourse. Before moving on to these chapters, however, I would first like to deal with the history of the feminist response to sentimentalism, which deserves detailed attention in its own right.

III. Mixed Feelings: "Extraordinary" Women and Traditional Feminist Criticism of the Sentimental

Janet Todd has commented that in the eighteenth century, "Sensibility fared badly with those wishing to improve women's position in society" (*Sensibility* 135). This insight holds true beyond the eighteenth century as well, since many feminist writers, including Mary Wollstonecraft, George Eliot, and Virginia Woolf, have been wary of an ideology that upholds both traditional religious values and the gender binaries of the domestic ideology. Even in more recent feminist criticism, scholars have been reluctant to embrace sentimentalism, not only because of the formal weaknesses so despised by literary critics, but because the ideology of the sentimental seems ultimately to weaken the social status of women.

Even in the eighteenth century, at the height of the Age of Sensibility, the feminist writer and thinker Mary Wollstonecraft was highly suspicious of the sentimental. As Janet Todd has suggested, Wollstonecraft's first novel, *Mary: A Fiction* (1788) was sympathetic to the sufferings of its sentimental heroine who escapes an unhappy marriage by throwing herself into charitable activities. By the time Wollstonecraft wrote *A Vindication of the Rights of Woman* (1798), however, she had come to believe that the system of sentimental education advocated by Rousseau constructed women as "weak, artificial beings" by making them slaves to their emotions (Wollstonecraft 81). She went on to argue that women must stop reading the sentimental novels that "work up stale tales, and describe meretricious scenes . . . in a sentimental jargon" and must start reading superior works that would "exercise the understanding and regulate the imagination" (306).

Wollstonecraft also resisted the idea that "women are supposed to possess more sensibility, and even humanity, than men" as evidenced by "their strong attachments and instantaneous emotions of compassion" (Wollstonecraft 312). She confronted and rejected the whole premise of sentimentalism, that women are "naturally" more compassionate and sympathetic; instead, she believed that this compassion, if it even exists, was not natural but the result of women's deficient education, "the natural consequence of [their] confined views" (312). Wollstonecraft maintained that women must abandon the deceptive ideals of sentimentalism and embrace severe rationality as the only way to reclaim their dignity and independence. In other words, she wanted women to reject the cultural values assigned to them by men, and embrace the "masculine" value of reason. Indeed, the whole argument of the *Vindication* is "to convince [women] that the soft phrases, susceptibility of heart, delicacy of sentiment, and refinement of taste, are almost synonymous with epithets of weakness" (81–82).

Wollstonecraft, therefore, rejected sentimentalism not only as a literary, but also as a social ideology, a viewpoint that was to be echoed in the nineteenth century by the Utilitarian political and social philosopher, John Stuart Mill, a supporter of women's rights. Mill echoed Wollstonecraft in his conviction that "What is now called the nature of women is an eminently artificial thing—the result of forced repression in some directions, unnatural stimulation in others" (38–39). The cause of this artificial "nature," according to Mill, is that:

> All women are brought up from the very earliest years in the belief that their ideal of character is the very opposite to that of men. . . . All the moralities tell them that it is the duty of women, and the all the current sentimentalities that it is their nature, to live for others . . . and to have no life but in their affections. (27)

On one hand, Mill's liberal position seems to be pro-woman: it touts the premise that, given half a chance, women could become as intelligent and capable as men and could fulfill a fully equal role in society. As Suzanne Clark has noted, however, one problem with Mill's liberal rationality as a model for feminism is that he divides women into two groups: "rational, free (masculine) individuals and inferior, unconscious individuals embedded in the matrix of feeling and ordinary life" (Clark 29). Even more importantly, though, Mill's ostensible liberalism also denigrates much of women's actual political and social activism in the nineteenth century.

It cannot be denied that the domestic ideology that Mill so deplored did encourage an important tradition of female charity—work which sometimes led to political activism, in such areas as factory and sanitary reform.[19] Mill particularly disapproved of these female charitable tendencies and philanthropic activities, which, he argued, were the result of "an education of the sentiments rather than of the understanding" (163). This sentimental education, according to the Utilitarian Mill, made women unable to see "the ultimate evil tendency of any form of charity or philanthropy which commends itself to their sympathetic feelings" (163). Mill's aversion to sentimental philanthropy was due to his conviction that "short-sighted benevolence ... saps the very foundations of the self-respect, self-help, and self-control which are the essential conditions both of individual prosperity and of social virtue" (163). He commended women's "insight ... into the minds and feelings of those with whom they are in immediate contact, in which women generally excel men," but said that women "born to the present lot of women" did not "appreciate the value of self-dependence" (164). In his distrust of female charity Mill showed that he was not an admirer of the actual political influence of the women of his time, which he claimed was marked only by "its aversion to war and its addiction to philanthropy" (162). Rather, he called for the development of 'extraordinary' women who could rise above the present lot of women and be, presumably, more like men.

The influence of this rejection of traditional femininity in favor of the idea of the extraordinary woman can be seen in feminist responses to sentimentalist literature. George Eliot, for example, wrote an influential essay called "Silly Novels By Lady Novelists" (1856) in which she ridiculed novels by her female contemporaries and urged women writers to aspire to higher standards of literary

---

[19]This is a thesis that is advanced by historian F.M. Prochaska in his book *Women and Philanthropy in Nineteenth-Century England* (Clarendon Press, 1980).

achievement. Singling out what she designated the "oracular" school of fiction—"novels intended to expound the writer's religious, philosophical, or moral theories"—for particular censure, she ranked these novels as "the most pitiable" of the silly novels by lady novelists (*Essays* 310). While Eliot never specifically classified social reform novels as oracular novels—in fact she even pointed out Elizabeth Gaskell and Harriet Beecher Stowe for particular commendation—the qualities that she criticized, namely the openly rhetorical, moralistic nature of these novels, were strikingly similar to the preachiness of social reform novels by women novelists. Significantly, Eliot did not praise Stowe for her social values or for her sympathy for the slaves she depicts, but for her realism: "Why can we not have pictures of religious life among the industrial classes of England, as interesting as Mrs. Stowe's pictures of religious life among the negroes?" (*Essays* 319).[20]

Some of Eliot's female contemporaries, notably the novelist and critic Dinah Mulock Craik, reproved Eliot for her departure from these more conventionally "feminine" fictional mores. In her review of Eliot's *Mill on the Floss* (1860), Craik argued that "the modern novel is one of the most important moral agents of the community" (442), and her critique of Eliot was based on that belief.[21] For although Craik conceded that *Mill on the Floss* was "as a work of art . . . is as perfect as a novel can well be made" (443), she believed that it fell short in its responsibility to "influence for good" (445) because of its failure to show Maggie overcoming temptation:

> It is not right to paint Maggie only as she is in her strong, unsatisfied, erring youth—and leave her there, her doubts unresolved, her passions unregulated, her faults unatoned and unforgiven; to cut her off ignobly and accidentally, leaving two acts, one her recoil of conscience with regard to Stephen, and the other her instinctive self-devotion in going to

---

[20]Christine Krueger has also suggested that "Eliot's criticisms of the abuses of 'oracularism' might also have been easily applied to many episodes in Gaskell's social problem fiction" (238).

[21]Mulock's review, "To Novelists—and a Novelist," appeared in *Macmillan's Magazine* in April, 1861.

> rescue Tom, as the sole noble landmarks of a life that had in it every capability for good with which a woman could be blessed. ("To Novelists—and a Novelist" 446–7)

For Craik, the moral responsibility of the novelist clearly prevailed over artistic considerations; she was representative of the "feminine" sentimentalist viewpoint in that she advocated a more rhetorical and moralistic idea of fiction.[22]

Craik's criticisms of *The Mill on the Floss* also reveal another unspoken, but evident, subtext behind this conflict: competing definitions of what it means not only to be a novelist, but, specifically, a woman novelist. Craik's review shows that she was very much aware of Eliot's gender. For instance, she put Eliot's male pseudonym in quotation marks, explaining that "we prefer to respect the pseudonym" (444). And, although Craik commended Eliot's "sexless intelligence" (446), Craik's 1858 book *A Woman's Thoughts About Women* demonstrated her own adherence to the 'separate spheres' philosophy: "No; equality of the sexes is not in the nature of things. Man and woman were made for, and not like one another" (13). She endorsed a woman's right "of having something to do" (13–14), but believed that these employments should conform to a woman's proper function—to be helpful, useful, and virtuous:

> Generally—and this is the best and safest guide—she will find her work lying very near at hand: some desultory tastes to condense into regular studies, some faulty household to quietly remodel, some child to teach, or parent to watch over. All these being needless or unattainable, she may extend her service out of the home into the world, which perhaps never at any time so much needed the help of us women. And hardly one of its charities and duties can be done so thoroughly as by a wise and tender woman's hand. (21)

---

[22]Richard Holt Hutton also seemed to have identified her as such when he featured Mulock in his attempt to define the strengths and weaknesses of woman novelists because "she represents more adequately the kind of faculty which is either potential or actual in most clever women" (468).

Interestingly enough, when Craik talked about literature as one possible employment for women, she was almost as severe as Eliot in her comments about women's writing, reserving her highest accolades for those such as Elizabeth Barrett Browning who pursued their writing "wholly, self-devotedly, and self-reliantly, . . . content with no height short of the highest" (51). Of the "secondary class" of women writers, "neither geniuses nor ordinary women—aspiring to both destinies, and usually achieving neither," she was surprisingly critical:

> But all who leave domestic criticism to plunge into the open arena of art—I use the word in its widest sense—must abide by art's severest canons. One of these is, that every person who paints a commonplace picture, or writes a mediocre book, contributes temporarily . . . to lower the standard of public taste, fills unworthily some better contributor's place, and without achieving any private good, does a positive wrong to the community at large. (52)

By the end of her discussion of "Female Professions," however, Craik concluded that every woman, even an artist, actress or singer, ought to be "the woman first, the *artiste* afterwards," since "our [women's] natural and happiest life is when we lose ourselves in the exquisite absorption of home, the delicious retirement of dependent love" (61-62). Since Craik so strongly supported this traditional viewpoint that assigned women the sentimental cultural values of sympathy and charity, it is not surprising that she should also have upheld sentimentalist ideas about fiction as well. Her own novels make use of sentimentalist emotionalism and they also conform to the more didactic, rhetorical nature of sentimentalist fiction, leading Richard Holt Hutton to remark that her novels suffer from too much "consciousness of sweet feeling" (481):

> The highest purpose has evidently guided Miss Muloch [sic] throughout her artistic career; and we are happy to observe its influence in a direction in which she is probably not fully conscious of it herself,— the clearing away of a certain vein of turbid rose-water sentiment which deluged "the Ogilvies" and is not imperceptible even in her best and ablest tales . . . . If she were less fond of nusing her sentiments,—dwelling on the 'fatal woman-heart,' and such like mawkish moods of thought,—

she might easily attain a far higher place in the literature of the day than she has ever yet reached. (481)

In contrast, the content of George Eliot's 1855 essay on Mary Wollstonecraft and Margaret Fuller shows Eliot's rejection of Craik's more traditional idea that women have greater access to sympathy and morality than men: she quoted Wollstonecraft's views on the subject at length, and said that both Wollstonecraft and Fuller had "too much sagacity to fall into this sentimental exaggeration" (*Essays* 205). In addition, although a useful study could probably be made of George Eliot's own use of sentimentalist attitudes and techniques in her fiction, such as in the moral perfection of Dinah Morris in *Adam Bede* (1859), it seems clear that in "Silly Novels by Lady Novelists," which led to her own literary career, she began the process of constructing herself as John Stuart Mill's "extraordinary" woman, who would rise above the "sentimental exaggeration" of conventional femininity that had hampered other female novelists.[23] In a sense, the vexed critical discourse that already surrounded the sentimental meant that Eliot could only achieve critical recognition by distinguishing herself from that important tradition of women's writing.

The same issues that colored Wollstonecraft's and Eliot's assessments of their contemporaries also have colored feminist critics' assessments of women's literary history. Virginia Woolf, for instance, spoke of having to "kill" the self-sacrificing, morally superior, Angel in the House before she could continue her writing career ("Professions for Women" 51–2).[24] What this rejection of

---

[23]Eliot's admiration for Margaret Fuller is also significant, since Fuller was consumed by a desire to be an extraordinary woman who would avoid the "sentimental tears" that marred her idols Madame de Stäel and George Sand: "Will there never be a being to combine a man's mind and a woman's heart, and who yet finds life to rich to weep over?" (Douglas 269).

[24]Elaine Showalter has convincingly characterized Woolf's own literary career as a "flight into androgyny. Although Woolf was deeply aware of a female tradition, "[she] was extremely sensitive to the ways in which female experience had made

conventional femininity has meant, though, is that a large portion of nineteenth-century writing by women has been forsaken not only by the male literary canon, but also by the feminist canon. Feminist scholars have too often rejected the conventional values that characterize sentimentalist fiction, and have either selected only the "best" female writers—Jane Austen, the Brontës, George Eliot, and Woolf herself—or have apologized for sentimentalist texts even while arguing for their importance.

In order to illustrate this point, I would like to discuss two important works of feminist criticism, both of which were published in 1977 at the height of the women's liberation movement. Elaine Showalter's well-known critical survey, *A Literature of Their Own*, attempts to construct a history of women's fiction in England from Brontë to Lessing, and Ann Douglas' more specific study, *The Feminization of American Culture*, analyzes the influence of sentimentalism in nineteenth-century American culture. The two works, in spite of their differences in subject matter, seem to be personally connected as well, since Showalter and Douglas thank each other in their acknowledgments. There are strong thematic similarities between these two studies in that both critics, while attempting to recognize the achievements of women writers, end up rejecting the conventional femininity of the sentimental in favor of a reduced tradition of acceptably feminist writers.

Showalter's study represents, above all, a paradox. While attempting to remedy the "residual Great Traditionalism" that has "reduced and condensed the extraordinary range and diversity of English women novelists to a tiny band of the 'great'" (7), Showalter herself constructs an evolutionary history of women's literature that ends up excluding the very "minor writers" she wishes to recover. Even the table of contents suggests a progression forward from the "feminine" novelists of the nineteenth century to the "feminist" novelists and so on, and Showalter's introduction explicitly outlines this evolution:

---

women weak, but much less sensitive to the ways in which it had made them strong" (*A Literature of Their Own* 285).

> First, there is a prolonged phase of imitation of prevailing modes of the dominant tradition, and internalization of its standards of art and its views on social roles. Second, there is a phase of protest against these standards and values . . . . Finally, there is a phase of self-discovery, a turning inward freed from some of the dependency of opposition, a search for identity. An appropriate terminology for women writers is to call these stages, Feminine, Feminist, and Female. (13)

This evolutionary model implies a rejection of the earlier "phases" of women's literary development, because it constructs the "feminine" novelists as the essentially weak and troubled precursors to a later, more admirable tradition. Showalter argues that these novelists struggled to define themselves by essentially male conceptions of femininity. Since women's work (as opposed to men's work) meant "work for others," the "feminine" novelists preached "submission and self-sacrifice, and by denouncing female self-assertiveness, they worked to atone for their will to write" (21–22).[25]

Even though Showalter often shows a great deal of insight, especially in her discussion of the nineteenth-century critical double standard, her evolutionary model implicitly privileges those women writers in whose works the feminine ideal is questioned or problematized—in other words, the 'extraordinary' women like Charlotte Brontë and George Eliot. Moreover, the subversion of the "feminine" novel that she identifies first in sensation fiction, and then in the activist feminist novels of the eighties and nineties, is clearly, in her timeline, a step forward from the "feminine" novel which had merely represented women's painful experience. Showalter's treatment of nineteenth-century fiction, therefore still privileges "the indispensable Jane and George," with the change that her Jane and George are Jane Eyre

---

[25]Showalter sees women's social-protest fiction both as an extension of this feminine ideal and as a kind of psychological projection which "translated the felt pain and oppression of women into the championship of mill-workers, child laborers, prostitutes, and slaves" (28).

and George Eliot rather than Jane Austen and George Eliot (Showalter 7).[26]

Unlike Showalter, Ann Douglas does not begin with any explicit intent to widen the literary canon, but *The Feminization of American Culture* starts out with the premise that an investigation of the sentimental "is crucial for understanding American culture in the nineteenth century and our own" (6). Such serious attention is an advance from the simple absence that had characterized previous scholarly opinion on the subject, and seems to open the door for the inclusion of these texts. While conceding that the sentimental is a valid subject for historical study, however, Douglas concludes that it had a profoundly negative effect on American culture and therefore ends up excluding sentimentalist texts even more firmly from the literary canon. She argues that women writers and readers debased American literary tastes and emasculated American religion from its rigorous Calvinist theology, resulting in an essentially dishonest and anti-intellectual mass culture. Explaining that these actions were not the result of deliberate, evil intent, she theorizes that the oppression and disestablishment of women in nineteenth-century culture was to blame: "Nineteenth-century American women were oppressed and damaged; inevitably, the influence they exerted in turn on their society was not altogether beneficial"(11).

Douglas herself privileges the "masculine "literary values of strength and toughness over the femininity of the sentimental. Although she claims to feel sympathy for the misguided women writers who colluded in their own downfall, her true sympathies are clearly with the male writers like Herman Melville, who were the victims of a nineteenth-century sentimental mass culture that failed to appreciate their works, and with "extraordinary" women like Margaret Fuller who resisted sentimentalism. Indeed, in Douglas' attitude towards sentimentalism's "debased religiosity" (6) and its confusion of "literature with self-justification" (9) there is a strong sense of frustration bordering on hatred—coupled with

---

[26] Showalter's version of the nineteenth century gives Brontë and Eliot noticeably more "air time" than any other individual writers.

what seems to be hatred of her own initial affection for sentimentalist fiction (3). For her, the feminization of American culture means that "America lost its male-dominated theological tradition without gaining a comprehensive feminism or an adequately modernized religious sensibility" (13). Douglas does not adequately address what these women may have gained from sentimentalism, and in the end, her book ends up re-ifying the traditional critical values that removed the sentimentalists from the literary canon in the first place. Even though it represents important research about a neglected group of writers, the study, in the final analysis, only sustains the essentially anti-feminist tradition of the "extraordinary" woman.

The issue of canonicity is of course an extremely vexed issue in feminist criticism, especially in attempts to find a female tradition. As Mary Eagleton points out in *Feminist Literary Theory*, this imperative to create a feminist canon can result in a failure to interrogate the idea of the canon itself:

> To talk of the female tradition of writing can reinforce the canonical view, which looks upon literary history as a continuum of significant names. Rather than disrupting the individualistic values by which the mainstream canon has been created, feminist critics sometimes merely replace a male First Eleven with a female one. . . . The very approach which has always seemed to find the majority of women writers lacking is transposed, uncritically, to a separate female tradition, and the humanist ethic which supports that approach is often acc epted as basically valid, merely in need of extending its franchise. (3–4)

In other words, Eagleton argues that feminist criticism has too often failed to force a total reconsideration of critical values and has replaced a male canon with a female one—simply reproducing the cultural Darwinism that narrowed the literary canon to begin with.

More recent critical works by Jane Tompkins, Suzanne Clark, and Nancy Armstrong represent some more productive directions for feminist literary criticism. I here refer to Jane Tompkins' *Sensational Designs* (1991), Suzanne Clark's *Sentimental Modernism* (1991), and Nancy Armstrong's *Desire and Domestic Fiction* (1987). Tompkins and Clark are important because, as I have demonstrated earlier in this chapter, they call previous critical judgments into question by historicizing them. Both Tompkins and Clark interrogate the idea of canonicity by arguing that the traditional idea of what makes a work "good" is the result of a certain historically bound ideological perspective. Tompkins uses this critical methodology to argue that certain previously excluded writers—namely sentimentalist domestic novels by nineteenth-century American women writers—ought to be rescued from their debased status as "weak-minded pap" and celebrated for their "intellectual complexity, ambition, and resourcefulness" (124). Clark uses her historicization of sentimentalism to specifically address the position of women writers in the modernist period, and then extends her argument to some contemporary women writers, such as Annie Dillard and Alice Walker, who, she argues, are still very much engaged with the sentimental. Since it avoids the Darwinian approach that ends up re-affirming "extraordinary" women writers and creating a parallel sub-canon of "minor" women writers, I believe that this kind of criticism represents a productive way to get women's literary productions into serious cultural circulation because it defies the supposedly objective critical standards that have been constructed largely by men.

I am convinced that Nancy Armstrong's work on the cultural work of eighteenth- and nineteenth-century British domestic fiction is also important, even though it does not explicitly make an argument for including excluded literary texts. Armstrong's Foucauldian understanding of power relations allows her to overcome the "rhetoric of victimization" that characterizes both Showalter and Douglas (255). Instead of working from a myth of female powerlessness, Armstrong suggests, feminists should focus on the ways that women's' cultural work constructed "a notion of the household as a specifically feminine space [which] established the preconditions for a modern institutional culture" (251). Although it does not explicitly address the literary canon as a theoretical issue, Armstrong's methodology presents a way of overcoming the myth of the 'extraordinary' woman by demonstrating the power of 'ordinary' women.

This book will present a revisionary look at nineteenth-century British fiction that addresses these ordinary women and their crucial cultural work that taught nineteenth-century audiences how to "read" and respond to social problems. I utilize Armstrong's Foucauldian understanding of power and the work of Tompkins and Clark on the historical construction of literary standards in order to demonstrate the largely unrecognized influence of a feminized, sentimentalist cultural discourse of social reform on nineteenth-century British culture. In the next chapter, I will therefore present a more materially situated explanation of sentimentalist discourse and its association with women writers. Further, I will then make an argument for the importance of Charlotte Elizabeth Tonna, a writer who represents the power and influence of sentimentalist discourse in nineteenth-century British culture.

Chapter Two

Preaching Pity: Women Writers and the Development of a Victorian Cultural Discourse of Social Reform

In this chapter, I describe the development of a cultural discourse of social reform that dominated nineteenth-century literature. Due chiefly to its reliance on feminized social and religious conventions such as emotionalism (otherwise known as sentimentality), direct address, religious didacticism, and biblical allusion, this sentimentalist cultural discourse has been pointedly ignored by the literary academy. Scholars need to recognize this discourse, however, as its practitioners—most, if not all, of whom were women—performed the crucial cultural work that taught nineteenth-century audiences to expect a new role for literature, and how to "read" and respond to social problems.

Many scholars, both historians and literary critics, have recognized that crucial shifts in cultural attitudes towards social issues like poverty occurred in the first few decades of the nineteenth century. The literature of the period reveals such shifts; pitiable victims of social problems in nineteenth-century novels like Dickens' *Bleak House* or Gaskell's *North and South* clearly do not belong in the abstract and comfortably ordered world of either earlier novelists like Jane Austen, or earlier social polemicists like Hannah More.[1] The later works both follow in the "feminine" tradition of sentimentalist discourse evident in writers like Charlotte Elizabeth Tonna and Frances Trollope; they are more emotionally engaging and morally strident because they reflect important changes in nineteenth-century structures of feeling.

---

[1] *Bleak House* was published serially in 1852–3, and *North and South* in 1854–5. The portrayals of characters like Jo, and Bessie Higgins, differ significantly from characterizations of poverty in More (1745–1833); such characters remain in the distant background in Jane Austen's fiction (1775–1817). For a good analysis of Austen's attitude towards the poor, see Beth Tobin's 1993 book, *Superintending the Poor*.

Cultural critic Raymond Williams uses the term "structure of feeling" to describe social attitudes and assumptions that go beyond formal ideology, encompassing cultural values as they are manifested, almost unconsciously, in popular culture and everyday life:

> It is not only that we must go beyond formally held and systematic beliefs, though of course we have always to include them. It is that we are concerned with meanings and values as they are actively lived and felt . . . characteristic elements of impulse, restraint, and tone; specifically affective elements of consciousness and relationships . . . (*Marxism and Literature* 132)

Williams' terms are particularly appropriate to this topic, which has everything to do with feeling. Sentimentalist novels tried to effect change by influencing the hearts and the feelings of their readers, exploiting the "feminine" cultural value of feeling for political purposes. This belief that feeling and emotion were the logical starting mechanisms for political change was exemplified by writers like Charlotte Elizabeth Tonna, in whose factory novel *Helen Fleetwood*,[2] one of the Lord Ashley-esque[3] factory reformers says, "I hope it may please God, before long, to rouse the *feelings* of our fellow countrymen on behalf of the poor children in these mills. If that was done, we should soon see a change for the better" (*Helen Fleetwood* 326, emphasis added). The rampant emotionalism of sentimentalist texts, the frequent deathbed scenes and portrayals of physical and emotional distress, the very qualities that often doom them to critical obscurity, were, in short, an integral part of their cultural work, work which was essential to the shifts in eighteenth- and nineteenth-century structures of feeling that made emotion and feeling politically meaningful.

Sentimentalist discourse also made skilled and impassioned use of commonly-held religious beliefs, beliefs that were believed

---

[2]*Helen Fleetwood* was published serially in *The Christian Lady's Magazine* from 1839–1840, and in volume form in 1841.

[3]Lord Ashley was a well known Evangelical, and a tireless advocate of humanitarian causes like factory and sanitary reform in Parliament.

to be the special province of women. These religious beliefs accounted for almost all of the discourse's most pertinent characteristics: from the urgently didactic "preacher" rhetoric that Christine Krueger has so helpfully analyzed in *The Reader's Repentance* (1992), to the flat characterizations drawn from the traditions of biblical typology, to, again, the ubiquitous deathbed scenes. When characters like Bessie Higgins, little Dick, and Helen Fleetwood died, they testified to "the reality of the life to come" and to all that this reality entails (Tompkins 129). Tonna, for instance, continually reminded her readers in her fiction and nonfiction that the world they know is subject to a higher power:

> Oh, it is an awful thought that so many believing, confiding prayers of the poor destitute are recorded in the book of HIS remembrance, whose piercing eye is never for one moment averted from the hidden plannings of the mercenary deceiver's heart! Very terrible will be the day of public inquisition and divine retribution. (*Helen Fleetwood* 42-43)

According to the system of eschatological Christian beliefs that guides the sentimentalist vision, the earthly world is subject to the cosmic order of a higher power, an order beginning with the Creation and ending with the Last Judgment. The work of writers like Tonna is suffused with the conviction that the world ought to conform to Biblical decree: " To us it ought to be enough that God has commanded us to care for the poor" (Tonna, *Perils of the Nation*, 123). The purpose of sentimentalist discourse was to influence the reader not only through pathos but through the whole "feminine" system of moral and religious values that the pathos epitomizes, a value system exemplified by both the urgent preaching of a narrator and emotional enactments of Christian eschatology.

The cultural prominence of fiction like Tonna's signalled important shifts in social attitudes and literary conventions—shifts that resulted in a new structure of feeling, a new cultural discourse. This sentimentalist discourse derived from two major factors: first, material conditions that necessitated the construction of a new, affective, morality in social reform discourse, and second, a domestic ideology that gave women "natural" dominance over both morality, and affect. Finally, I will go on to demonstrate the changes resulting from these two factors with a contrast between the work of eighteenth-century evangelist Hannah More, and that of her nineteenth-century "disciple" Charlotte Elizabeth Tonna, who I believe to have been one of the key figures in the construction of this sentimentalist cultural discourse.

I. The Death of the Moral Economy: Social Change and the Need for a New Cultural Discourse

Even in the eighteenth-century, social and economic changes like enclosure, the disenfranchisement of the small farmer, the growing poverty of laborers, and population shifts from rural areas to urban areas, signalled the slow death of what historian E.P. Thompson has termed the "moral economy," a traditional, paternal social system based on complex social relationships of trust, deference, and obligation.[4] In a historical study of the eighteenth-century grain market, Thompson argues that eighteenth-century food riots, were expressions of "a popular consensus...of the proper economic functions of several parties within the community, which...can be said to constitute the moral economy of the poor"("Moral Economy" 78–9). He demonstrates that an older paternalist system existing in "an eroded body of Statute law, as well as common law and custom," enforced an economy of provision in which the primary responsibility of the food producers was to meet the needs of their immediate community, even to the detriment of their own profits. This moral economy assumed the existence of a tightly-woven community, in which all members, both producers and consumers, were responsible to each other; the local farmers, millers, and bakers, under this system, were under obligation to meet the needs of their neighbors, to "provision" in other words, at a price the local consumers could pay. Thompson maintains that in the eighteenth-century, a new, more impersonal, money-based, market economy, "disinfested

---

[4]Also see Beth Tobin, who argues that these changes signalled the "passing of the old society's paternal social and economic relations" (*Superintending the Poor* 8–9).

[sic] of intrusive moral imperatives," gradually replaced this older moral economy, and that the food riots expressed popular indignation over the change (90).

The death of the moral economy did not just result from the victory of one economic theory over another, however, but from a complex network of social and economic changes, by which England evolved from a rural nation of small, tightly knit communities to an industrial and urban nation. Historian Francis Sheppard states that at the beginning of the nineteenth century, three quarters of the population of England and Wales still lived in the country, or in towns with a population under 20,000, while by 1871, this proportion had fallen to less than half. Raymond Williams also gives a thumbnail sketch of this process of change in *The Country and the City*, linking a rising number of displaced people in the countryside caused by the practice of enclosure, to a corresponding growth of population in the cities as the new industrial system of production demanded workers. Finally, Williams contends, "The crisis of poverty, which was so marked in towns and villages alike in the late eighteenth and early nineteenth centuries, was a result of this social and economic process as a whole" (98).[5]

---

[5]Even conservative historian Gertrude Himmelfarb admits in *The Idea of Poverty*:

> However one may qualify the idea of an agricultural or industrial "revolution," there can be no doubt of the enormity of the changes in the countryside and towns. There were fewer "deserted villages" than the poets thought, but many depressed ones; fewer large cities by later standards, but many rapidly growing ones with all the problems they brought in their wake. (Himmelfarb 135)

Himmelfarb qualifies this link between these social changes and increased poverty, with her statement that other problems, such as poor harvests and the Napoleonic wars, created economic problems. I am, of course, more interested in the perception of a previous "moral economy," than in arguing about whether this social shift really existed or not, but the fact that a conservative historian like Himmelfarb admits, however grudgingly, the

Although Williams refuses to characterize these social changes as "the substitution of one [social] order for another" (98), it is clear that contemporary writers, observing the growing separation of social classes, perceived the gradual disappearance of a traditional system, namely the moral economy, as a contributing cause to the crisis of poverty. Many observers lamented the moral breakdown caused by class separation and the disappearance of community in the late eighteenth century and early nineteenth century, and these accounts increased in the eighteen-thirties and forties, when the migration of people from the countryside to London and to the factory towns seemed to bring the situation to a state of crisis.[6] Most nineteenth-century scholars are familiar with Friedrich Engels' famous observation of this phenomenon in Manchester in *The Condition of the Working Class in England* (1844):

> Owing to the curious lay-out of the town it is quite possible for someone to live for years in Manchester and to travel daily to and from his work without ever seeing a working class quarter or coming into contact with an artisan. He who visits Manchester simply on business or for pleasure need never see the slums, mainly because the working-class districts and the middle class districts are quite distinct. (Engels 54)

In London itself, the construction of railways at mid-century facilitated the middle- and upper-class move to the suburbs that intensified "the social differentiation of the various parts of London" (Sheppard 8), but it is clear that this process of class separation was already well underway even before that, provoked by the rapid expansion that led William Cobbett to call London an "infernal Wen" in 1822.[7] James Grant asserted in 1842 that

---

existence of a previous social order, and even uses the term "moral economy" in her analysis, gives credence to the arguments of Marxist historians and critics like E. P. Thompson and Raymond Williams.

[6]See Beth Tobin's discussion of eighteenth-century writings on these social problems in *Superintending the Poor* (1993), pp. 8–9.

[7]The population of Cobbett's home parish of Kensington increased from 14,000 in 1821 to 120,000 in 1871 (Sheppard 83–84).

"[t]he great mass of the metropolitan community are as ignorant of the destitution and distress which prevail in large districts of London...as if the wretched creatures were living in the very centre of Africa" (Dyos 135).[8] This phenomenon closely resembles Engels' descriptions of Manchester, and the similarity suggests that all of Britain's cities were probably characterized by this same physical separation of classes. This conclusion is also supported by urban historian H. J. Dyos, who notes that "the bulk of the annals of the slums between the 1840's and the beginning of the 1880's are basically of this type, social reportage that was meant to supply unpleasant facts to those unlikely to obtain them for themselves" (Dyos 134).

For the purposes of this book, I am interested in the perception of the moral economy's breakdown, particularly as it affects the cultural discourses of the eighteen-thirties and forties. This perception exists not only in historical observers like Engels, but also in literary discourse, and the two became, in some ways, inseparable. One example of this phenomenon is the critical reception of Dickens' *Oliver Twist* (1837–9), in which the rookeries where Fagin's gang and Bill Sikes live are, quite literally, portrayed as "hideouts" where middle-class values and institutions can only penetrate with difficulty. Dickens imports a virtual army of policemen and a mob suffused with righteous indignation in order to bring the criminals, Bill Sikes and Fagin to justice. Sikes is finally hunted down in Jacob's Island, a slum that Dickens calls "the filthiest, the strangest, the most extraordinary of the many localities that are hidden in London, wholly unknown, even by name, to the great mass of its inhabitants" (*Oliver Twist* 442).

The influence of this literary portrayal of Jacob's Island on the public imagination was illustrated in 1850, when at a meeting of the Metropolitan Sanitary Association both the Bishop of London

---

[8]By the 1890s, when sociologist Charles Booth made his famous survey of *The Life and Labour of the People of London*, Booth's maps—in which districts were color-coded according to income level—reveal lower-income districts surrounded by a "camouflage" of commercial property, and separated distinctly from higher-income districts.

and Dickens himself made speeches in which they called attention to the problem of sanitary conditions in poor districts by making references to Jacob's Island. A week later, when the Marylebone Vestry was debating whether to use tax money to educate poor children, Dickens' enemy Sir Peter Laurie[9] took the opportunity not only to oppose this measure, but to attack reformers in general, reading the passage about Jacob's Island from the Bishop's speech at the Sanitary Association meeting, and saying, "The Bishop of London, poor soul . . . in his simplicity, thought there really was such a place . . . whereas it turned out that it only existed in a work of fiction, written by Mr. Charles Dickens ten years ago" (Dickens, *Speeches* 108–9).[10] Historian Gareth Stedman-Jones, in fact, blames Dickens and other literary figures, such as G.M.W. Reynolds and Henry Mayhew, for the ruthless slum clearance projects of the mid-nineteenth century, and condemns them for exploiting and sensationalizing the living conditions of the poor (Stedman-Jones 180).

The real significance of the Dickens/Laurie anecdote, however, is that it highlights the additional function(s) that cultural discourse, and particularly fictional discourse, came to fulfill in this new social environment. Laurie was able to argue that Jacob's Island didn't exist because, clearly, no one in his audience had ever been there, and had only experienced the slum through the medium of Dickens' fiction.[11] Engels and other observers

---

[9]Dickens had satirized Laurie in his characterization of the hypocritical Alderman Cute in *The Chimes* (1845).

[10]Sheila Smith's book on nineteenth-century literary portrayals of the poor, *The Other Nation* (1980), describes this episode at length.

[11]Jacob's Island was also described by Charles Kingsley in *Alton Locke* (1850), by Henry Mayhew in an 1849 *Morning Chronicle* article on "The Cholera Districts of Bermondsey," and by J. Saunders in an 1841–4 collection of essays on London edited by Charles Knight. Dickens' original description was so dominant, however, that Saunders simply quoted it, saying "the features . . . are described with such close accuracy . . . that we cannot do better than quote the passage" (Smith 66).

commented on the disastrous moral effects of class separation, which made it easier for the wealthier strata of society to ignore the appalling living and working conditions of the poor. As W. Cooke Taylor complained in 1842, "We have improved on the proverb, 'One half of the world does not know how the other half lives,' changing it into 'One half of the world does not care how the other half lives'" (qtd. in Thompson, *The Making of the English Working Class* 322). Since middle-class Victorian readers were increasingly isolated from the suffering caused by social problems, often the only contact they themselves would have with this suffering would be through the medium of written discourse, usually through fiction. Fiction, then, became the principal medium by which affective bonds were constructed between different social groups. This function was primarily identified with and performed by women authors, who fought their audience's indifference and desensitization to suffering with the culturally sanctioned emotionalism of their writing.

II. The "Two Nations" and the Woman Writer

> "Two nations; between whom there is no intercourse and no sympathy; who are as ignorant of each other's habits, thoughts, and feelings, as if they were dwellers in different zones, or inhabitants of different planets; who are formed by a different breeding, are fed by a different food, are ordered by different manners, and are not governed by the same laws."
> "You speak of—" said Egremont, hesitatingly.
> "THE RICH AND THE POOR."
>
> —Benjamin Disraeli, *Sybil* (1842)

By the eighteen-forties, the idea that the rich and the poor were two opposing camps, isolated from each other, dominated cultural discourse. The perceived need to construct affective bonds between these two groups created a new function for many women authors, who, because of their culturally sanctioned roles as guardians of "sympathy" and "mutual understanding" ("The Lady Novelists of Great Britain" 24) came to figure prominently in the arena of social reform literature. The nineteenth-century reading public came to accept, even to expect, that literary works, particularly novels, would address issues like slavery, poverty, working and housing conditions, prostitution, and so on, and equally to expect women to be the authors of these novels.

It also became a widely accepted cultural truism that novels had an important influence over the reading public, to the great concern of conservative literary critics like the *National Review*'s W. R. Greg, who lamented "The False Morality of Lady Novelists" in 1859. These critics operated within a well established nineteenth-century critical trope that defined novels as "light literature," and therefore feminine, and characterized novel reading as "addictive, sensational, and irresponsible" (Ferris 18). As the title of Greg's review suggests, its main purpose was to deplore the moral influence that novels had on their readers, and to condemn the "fantastic and flatulent morality" of "sentimental" women novelists (158).

A few years later, in 1864, a *Westminster Review* critic commented that novelists were also politically influential, because of their ability to reach a wide audience:

> The novelist is now our most influential writer . . . . The influence of the novelist is beginning, too, to be publicly acknowledged of late more frankly than was once the fashion. For a long time his power over society, except as a mere teller of stories and provider of easy pastime, was ignored or disputed. It was, indeed, something like the power of women in politics; an influence almost all-pervading, almost irresistible, but silent, secret, and not to be openly acknowledged. ("Novels With a Purpose" 27–28)

Both Greg and the *Westminster Review* critic expressed anxiety about the influence of novels, and the source of this anxiety reveals itself both in the title of Greg's review and in the last sentence of the anonymous review, which compares the influence of the novel to the "power of women in politics." Even a cursory glance at the history of nineteenth-century British social reform literature shows that novels by women were an important political presence, one not to be underestimated. Joseph Kestner's 1985 book *Protest and Reform* catalogues the overwhelming presence of women writers in the history of nineteenth-century British social protest fiction. Kestner argues that women writers actually dominated this subgenre of literature, which gave them a great deal of political and cultural authority (213).

One such politically influential woman was the Evangelical editor and novelist, Charlotte Elizabeth Tonna. Tonna was the editor of the influential *Christian Lady's Magazine* from 1834–1846 and *The Protestant Annual* from 1841–46, and author of several fictional works, including an anti-slavery novel, *The System* (1827); an indictment of the factory system, *Helen Fleetwood* (1839–40); an exposure of the abuses of women and children laborers in *The Wrongs of Woman* (1843–44); and the nonfictional *Perils of the Nation* (1843), which repeats many of the themes and ideas in the fictional works. Tonna's prestige, as the editor of *The Christian Lady's Magazine*, and as the author of an influential novel on factory issues in *Helen Fleetwood*, inspired the Christian Influence Society to ask her in 1842 to write a study of the condition of Britain, which resulted in the anonymously published *Perils of the Nation*. Tonna's husband recalled after her death that: "The book...had a marked and decided influence, not only on the tone of public feeling, but directly on the Legislature, admits of no doubt. It was quoted on platforms and discussed in private circles . . ." (Krueger 151).[12] Although *Perils* itself was published anonymously, Tonna would not have been asked to write it if her fiction had not already given her a degree of political influence, and it is this female political influence, introduced insidiously

---

[12]Tonna published the work under the name of her longtime publisher, Richard Seeley, who published *The Christian Lady's Magazine*, and Tonna's own *Helen Fleetwood* and *Personal Recollections*. I suspect that Tonna's well-known affiliation with Seeley, as well as her well-known involvement in factory reform, probably meant that her authorship of *Perils* was not as unknown to her contemporaries as it was to become to twentieth-century literary critics and historians. As recently as 1982, historian H.J. Dyos' *Exploring the Urban Past* attributed *Perils* to Seeley; it was not until feminist literary critic Joseph Kestner researched Tonna extensively for his book *Protest and Reform* (1985), that she was correctly identified as the author of *Perils*.

through the medium of fiction into "private circles," that disturbed critics like Greg and the *Westminster Review* writer.

In spite of the prominence of women novelists in the arena of social reform, most of the literary criticism on the subject of novelist as social polemicist has focused on male novelists, particularly the most popular and influential of nineteenth-century novelists, Charles Dickens. Although some other figures, such as Elizabeth Gaskell, Charles Kingsley, and Benjamin Disraeli are mentioned, the critical discussion tends to focus on Dickens as the writer who, in the words of Karl Marx, "issued to the world more political and social truths than have been uttered by all the professional politicians, publicists and moralists put together" (Ackroyd 720).[13] This intense focus on Dickens does not give an accurate picture of nineteenth-century cultural discourse, however, because it exaggerates Dickens' originality. Dickens—dubbed "Mr. Popular Sentiment" by his fellow novelist Anthony Trollope—was a writer whose greatest skill lay in his ability to meet his readers' expectations. As his most recent biographer Peter Ackroyd puts it: "there never was a writer more adept at judging his readership than Charles Dickens. He knew precisely what effect to achieve, and precisely the means with which to do it" (Ackroyd 856).

As I will show at greater length in the next chapter of this book, much of Dickens' effectiveness as a popular novelist and social reformer was dependent on sentimentalist conventions, and by extension on his audience's comprehension and acceptance of these conventions. In other words, the pathos and preachiness of works like *A Christmas Carol* were effective only because its audience already knew how to "read" Tiny Tim and the other scenes that the three Spirits use to convert Scrooge. If the success of Dickens, and of other important mid-century literary figures like Elizabeth Gaskell and Elizabeth Barrett Browning, was dependent on what seem to be accepted cultural conventions, then this success indicates the existence of a now largely unknown

---

[13]In fact, Ackroyd's misuse of this quotation proves my point, since Marx's original statement referred not only to Dickens, but also to Dickens' fellow British novelists, Elizabeth Gaskell and Charlotte Brontë.

sentimentalist cultural discourse that would account for such conventions. In fact, this discourse did exist, but its dominant figures, women writers such as Frances Trollope, Elizabeth Stone, Camilla Toulmin, and finally the most politically influential, Charlotte Elizabeth Tonna, have been almost entirely forgotten. They are, in the words of the anonymous *Westminster Review* critic, the "influence almost all-pervading, almost irresistible, but silent, secret, and not to be openly acknowledged" ("Novels With a Purpose" 28).

This exclusion was largely due to the high-culture backlash against sentimentalism that I detailed in the previous chapter, in which the increasingly aesthetic literary standards of the nineteenth-century became even more severe with the advent of formalist New Criticism. Even at the turn of the century before the advent of New Criticism, Louis Cazamian disparaged the emotionalism of Tonna's fiction—"her inner passion was a matter of sentiment, rather than will or intellect"—although he also commended its "deeply sincere and weighty seriousness" (237).[14] In other words, while he conceded that Tonna's writing was effective—"moving and persuasive"—Cazamian denied that it was artistic (239). The same feminized elements that made the writing of women social reform writers effective and culturally acceptable, in effect, also denied it any kind of artistic status.

Cazamian's a-historical statement also failed to take into account the cultural imperatives that informed Tonna's "sentiment." As Ann Cvetkovich claims, "the assumptions that affective expression forms the basis for political action and itself constitutes a political act derive from a nineteenth-century discourse that made affect meaningful." This discourse, Cvetkovich argues, results from "the gendered division between the private and public spheres and the assignment of women to the affective tasks of the household" (Cvetkovich 6). This analysis derives in part from feminist critic Nancy Armstrong's explanation of the eighteenth- and nineteenth-century domestic

---

[14]For many years, Cazamian's 1903 study, *The Social Novel in England: 1830–1870*, was considered to be the authoritative work on nineteenth-century social reform fiction in England.

ideology: "According to the middle-class ideal of love . . . the female relinquishe[d] political control to the male in order to acquire exclusive authority over domestic life, emotions, taste, and morality," creating a "sexual contract" that gave women control over morals and affect (Armstrong 41). Armstrong quotes Frederick Rowton's introduction to his 1848 anthology of women poets in order to elaborate on this gendered "division of labor" (93) as it applies to literature:

> Man has to bear outward, tangible rule; and his faculties are necessarily of an authoritative, evident, external commanding order. Woman has to bear invisible sway over the hidden mechanism of the heart; and her endowments are of a meek, persuasive, quiet, and subjective kind. Man rules the mind of the world; woman its heart. (Armstrong 40)

The gendered separation of powers does give women influence, but only over emotional matters, "the heart," and morality, as is shown when Rowton writes later in his preface that the poems in his anthology do not "accelerate man's political advancement; whilst every page will display some effort to stimulate his moral progress" (Armstrong 41). Rowton's preface also indicates—through the use of phrases like "Man has to. . ." and "Woman has to. . ."—the extent to which this domestic ideology was naturalized in nineteenth-century culture, to the point that it was not a choice but an imperative of nature.[15]

This domestic ideology made it possible—indeed, almost necessary—for women writers, coming from their "naturally" more emotional and spiritual perspective, to construct a cultural discourse of social reform based on these feminine qualities, and to become identified with it. In spite of the reviewers' more narrow interpretation of the domestic ideology, which saw female forays into political discourse as a highly suspect, women writers like Charlotte Elizabeth Tonna perceived their roles differently. Seizing upon the political potential implicit within the domestic ideology,

---

[15]As I demonstrated with my discussions of George Henry Lewes, Richard Holt Hutton, and even Dinah Mulock Craik in the previous chapter, Rowton's generalization was representative of many nineteenth-century literary critics.

they used its imperatives to become the "natural" authors of a discourse that would create affective bonds between the "two nations" divided by the disappearance of the moral economy. In fact, this partnership of gender and politics was so strong, that women writing on the other side of the "Condition of England" debate, in favor of Political Economy, could be labelled as "unfeminine." For instance, in *Perils of the Nation*, Tonna criticized Harriet Martineau's *Illustrations of Political Economy* (1834) as one of the "Errors of the Day:"

> Ladies, no doubt, have a particular liberty of speech, and a comparative immunity from harsh reprisals, when they express in their own persons the opinions they may have imbibed: but when a lady creates a . . . mouthpiece of the most revolting principles, we cannot extend over him the shield that covers his fair inventress: however we may and do lament the perversion of a female mind to aid in so bad, so unfeminine a cause. (157)

Moreover, as I suggested in the previous chapter of this book, there was some support from the larger culture for this more active role. In an 1853 issue of *The Gentleman's Magazine*, for example, a reviewer trying to assess the achievement of "The Lady Novelists of Great Britain" explicitly designated this affective task as one especially suited to women novelists:

> At this day there is a strong prevailing disposition put forth, not before it was needed, to look after our outcasts of all sorts . . . Something there may be of sentimentality, something of the love of excitement, in this: but let no one neglect or throw contempt on the impulse which leads the higher classes—high whether in the social or the moral scale—to communicate freely with the lower. . . . our literature and our morals require more and more for their basis a sound increasing knowledge and sympathy between all orders of men. Mutual comprehension—mutual understanding of each other, how inestimable a privilege it is! This is what women can especially forward. . . . (*"The Lady Novelists of Great Britain"* 24)

Therefore, this identification of women with "sympathy" and "sentiment"[16] did create a political function for women, although

---

[16] The review uses both of these words several times.

it theoretically kept them contained within the domestic sphere. The reviewer in *The Gentleman's Magazine* even sanctioned this political role when he commended the French novelist George Sand and Harriet Beecher Stowe for their novels on political issues:

> With the means of high religious and moral cultivation within her reach ... why should not a woman write fiction admirably well? Bear witness to a woman's power, most wonderful Consuelo! Stand forward, earnest, inspired, duteous, magnanimous "Uncle Tom," and say what there is, what long-standing system of wickedness, that may not be shaken to its centre by the touch of a woman's hand! (*The Gentleman's Magazine* 19)

The domestic ideology, then, gave women writers a social/political function that was not only for women in literature, but to some extent, to women in the outside world.[17] Historian F.M. Prochaska has noted the domination of women in nineteenth-century charitable work, to the extent that "organized philanthropy had become 'womanized' in the nineteenth century" (223). This power, however, was inextricably linked to the "sentiment," and the "high religious and moral cultivation" that were so dubious to literary critics.[18]

III. "The Talent of Female Influence": The Power of Sentimental Morality

At the beginning of this chapter, I referred to significant differences between sentimentalist fiction and the work of earlier writers like Hannah More. I would now like to define these differences, and describe the development of sentimentalist

---

[17]Cazamian echoed these sentiments when he linked women writers with the success of Christian interventionism: "it was left to women's gentler and more impulsive imaginations to mark the link between the charitable precepts of Christianity and the duty of social responsibility" (212).

[18]Even the *Gentleman's Magazine* reviewer, while celebrating "woman's championship on social questions" (18), qualified his literary judgment of this championship by saying "[s]omething there may be of sentimentality ... in this ..." (24).

cultural discourse with an analysis of the transition between Tonna's friend and mentor, the eighteenth-century evangelist and social commentator, Hannah More, and Tonna's own work. Tonna considered her relationship with More to have been one of the greatest influences on her public career—and the two writers certainly had a great deal in common. Both women were politically conservative, intensely pious, and extremely skillful at manipulating the ideology and rhetoric of evangelism to shape social discourse.

There are significant differences in the ways that the two deal with social issues, however, as literary critic Catherine Gallagher acknowledges in *The Industrial Reformation of English Fiction* (1985) when she says that Tonna's characters in *Helen Fleetwood* "are not characters who could have been imagined by Hannah More" (50–1), but Gallagher confines her insight to the issue of free will and determinism in industrial fiction. Tonna's innovations from More are more important than that because they show the development of a cultural discourse that responded to cultural conditions generated both by the new material circumstances that came with the industrial era, and by a domestic ideology that gave women a specific political and social function to enact within those material conditions.

Tonna particularly admired More's *Cheap Repository Tracts* (1795–8), a collection of short political and religious pamphlets, as "an enterprise worthy of especial note" because of its "effective championship of the good cause [the Anglican church], by means most admirably suited to its furtherance" (*Personal Recollections* 210).[19] One of More's tracts, "The Lancashire Collier Girl," tells the story of the devastation experienced by one family caught up in the beginning phases of the Industrial Revolution. The

---

[19]Tonna obviously admired More's adaptation of fiction as a political and religious tool, and More's works overcame Tonna's prejudice against fiction. In general, Tonna disapproved of fiction (see *Personal Recollections*), but it became acceptable when used for a "good cause," like More's advocacy of the Anglican church, or Tonna's own later use of fiction for causes such as factory reform and poor relief.

heroine, Mary, loses her father to an industrial accident, her mother and brothers to overwork and malnutrition, and nearly dies herself before she is "rescued" by the local gentry. More addresses her audience simply and directly, often stopping in her narrative to prescribe meanings to be inferred from the events she relates. After Mary's father is killed, for instance, More tells her readers, "I will here remark that the most grievous afflictions are often appointed by Providence to be the means, in one way or other, of calling some extraordinary virtue into exercise" (More, vol. 5, 144).[20] This directly stated religious didacticism, or "preachiness," is one element that early evangelical writers like More contributed to sentimentalist discourse whose "stated purpose," as literary critic Jane Tompkins explains, "is to influence history, and which therefore employ[s] a language... common and accessible to everyone" (125).

More's didacticism, however, lacked the more urgent religious imperatives that give sentimentalism its force. Thrust forward by the cultural conditions created by the death of the moral economy, Tonna drove her message of charity home by vehement biblical references like this one from *The Wrongs of Woman*:

> He, the LORD, who changes not, looks down from the height of his glory on the very humblest of his handmaidens toiling below, no less benignantly than in the days of his flesh... How, then, dwelleth the love of Christ in us, if we connive at the cruel oppression exercised over the helpless young females of our land? (107)

In *The Perils of the Nation*, Tonna used the same attitude of religious judgment to argue that England, as a Christian nation, should conform to the laws of God:

> God looks down from heaven upon the children of men, whose frame he well knows, and whom he never willingly afflicts or grieves; each one of whom he sent into the world naked and helpless, and each one of whom in nakedness and helplessness must stand before him at the great day [of

---

[20]For the purposes of this book, I used an eight-volume edition of the *Cheap Repository Tracts*, distributed by the American Tract Society. No publication date is given, but the illustrations indicate that the edition is mid-nineteenth-century.

judgment]; and what a spectacle does he behold! Not among savage and barbarous nations, who never heard of the great Creator and his laws, of the blessed Redeemer and his love . . . but in a country where the knowledge of his will in all things is attainable by every human being who enquires concerning it, does this [factory] system exist. (20)

Clearly, Tonna recognized little or no distinction between spiritual and civil law, and as far as she was concerned, those in power needed to behave as representatives not only of civil, elected authority, but also of divine authority. Later in the same text, she addressed the members of Parliament: "We would not wilingly believe concerning any man that he held the future judgment of God so light a thing as to be braved for a little present gain" (242). Both of the passages by Tonna contain two themes in common: first, the eschatological certainty that present actions will be subject to future divine judgment, and second, that divine (Biblical) pronouncements are innately superior to earthly laws and socially accepted codes of behavior. Unlike More's, Tonna's Christianity urged her readers to share in its eschatological expectations and its moral judgments—it portrayed contemporary events as parts of the transcendental history revealed in the Bible, and as therefore subject to the same divine laws. In fact, it implied that God will wrathfully punish those readers who fail to pity the poor and helpless a message which was never present in More's tracts.

More's "The Lancashire Collier Girl" did appeal somewhat to the Christian values of its audience in that it argued that the rich should take some responsibility for showing charity and fairness to the poor, but her moral and philosophical framework seemed to assume that upper-class readers were already aware of this responsibility. The primary message of "The Lancashire Collier Girl," and of More's other celebrated tracts like "The Shepherd of Salisbury Plain," was to lower-class readers, who were told to practice the virtues of self-help, to be patient and submissive, and to "do their duty in that state of life, into which it hath pleased God to call them" (More, vol. 5, 155). Upper-class readers, on the other hand, were not as stridently instructed in their responsibilities, with a few exceptions such as the end of "The Lancashire Collier Girl," where they are told "not to turn the poor from their doors, merely on account of first appearances, but rather first to examine into their character, expecting sometimes to find peculiar modesty and merit, even in the most exposed situations" (More, vol. 5, 154).

Charlotte Elizabeth Tonna's most important innovation from More is the way that she described the physical and emotional suffering of her subjects in detail. Like More, Tonna did distance herself from eighteenth-century sentimental morality in *Perils of the Nation* when she claimed that "Tenderness for the poor is not among the spontaneous impulses of man's evil heart; if that were so, we should not find line upon line . . . enjoining it in the word of God" (186). However, her works contain so many heart-wrenching scenes of suffering, clearly meant to influence her audience's emotions, that the actual content of her works belies that claim. Her factory novel, *Helen Fleetwood*, was intended to call attention to the plight of the factory workers, and to denounce the factory system and the way that the Utilitarian-sponsored New Poor Law forced destitute people into the factories as laborers. The novel tells the story of Widow Green, and her orphaned grandchildren, who are driven from their country home by the pressures of the New Poor Law and forced to work in one of the textile mills in the town of M (Manchester). Mrs. Green's other married daughter, Mrs. Wright, already lives with her family in M, and has four children who have worked in the factories since early childhood. Long passages in the novel describe how factory labor has warped these children, physically, mentally, and emotionally, but the most injured is the oldest daughter Sarah:

> The girl who occupied a low chair near the chimney-corner appeared to be naturally much taller than Phoebe [her younger sister], but was so twisted and crooked that she scarcely reached her height. Every feature betokened consumption far advanced; and her large glassy grey eyes seemed to rove about in quest of some object to interest them; while an expression of melancholy discontent shewed how vain was the search. A large shawl pinned close round the throat fell over her shoulders and body; and she evidently was as helpless as an infant. (*Helen Fleetwood* 71)

This passage not only gives a detailed physical description of Sarah, but also invites the reader to put him or herself in Sarah's place, to feel her physical helplessness and the mental and spiritual destruction caused by her condition. Later passages in the novel portray the psychological and spiritual dynamics of Sarah's unhappy family situation, and further the reader's identification with her. Similar passages in Tonna and in the works of other nineteenth-century sentimentalist authors gave detailed physical and emotional accounts of consumptive seamstresses, malnourished factory workers, deformed child laborers, and so forth. Such passages were obviously meant to dramatize suffering, and represent "social problems as affective dilemmas"—in other words, as matters of the heart (Cvetkovich 2).

This move, of course, put social problems squarely within the realm of the feminine and made use of the domestic ideology, which gave women control over morality and emotion. Tonna specifically appealed to that ideology countless times in her writings, even as early as the beginning of her editorship of *The Christian Lady's Magazine* in 1834, when she justified her monthly political editorials with the following:

> Can we write for CHRISTIAN LADIES, and be guiltless, if we neglect to enforce upon them their high responsibility, in the use of that mighty talent, female influence? . . . It is when his [man's] home becomes the abode of gentle sympathy and intellectual companionship, and spiritual communion, that man begins to feel that he has somewhat worth fencing around . . . And thus . . . does the talent of female influence form the basis of even all commercial intercourse among the nations of the earth. (*Christian Lady's Magazine*, vol. 1, 249–50)

In this passage, Tonna carefully restrained the woman's influence to the home, in accordance with the domestic ideology, but she constructed this domestic role in a way that includes, even demands, the "high responsibility" of moral activism.

Tonna also referred to female influence in *Helen Fleetwood* in a specifically political form, as an impetus towards legislative factory reform:

> Now suppose a lady . . . looking upon her own children and thinking what she should feel if they were situated like the wretched little ones in the factories . . . . don't you think these ladies would use their influence

> over their own husbands, fathers, brothers, and friends, to make it a point with the candidate they vote for that he should support our cause in Parliament? (*Helen Fleetwood* 326)

This passage is particularly significant because it shows how important sympathy, or affect, was in causing the changes of heart that would, in turn, result in the women's influence over their men. Even in *The Perils of the Nation*, which was anonymous and therefore comparatively genderless, there is this direct appeal to women's influence. The last section of *Perils* consists of a series of appeals for action on social reform, directed towards the various segments of society (Parliament, the Ministers of the Crown, the Church of England bishops and clergy, magistrates, the legal and medical professions, etc.), and it is probably no accident that the very last of these appeals is to female influence, "mighty for good or ill" (345). It is clear that Tonna considered affective morality to be feminine, and equally clear that it was crucial to her concept of her own efficacy as a writer and reformer.

Hannah More, on the other hand, seemed determined to deflect the pity and emotion of the audience in "The Lancashire Collier Girl," rather than to arouse it. The text of the tract glosses over the deaths of Mary's father, mother, and brothers, and the narrator describes the heroine Mary's own illness with an absolute minimum of detail, only saying that "she began to be bowed down in some measure by the afflictions which she had endured" (More, vol. 5, 148). The narrator immediately goes on to observe "how lamentable a thing is it, that while so many people are seen who are apt to complain too soon, there should be any who do not tell their distresses to those who can help them. . ." (149). More's constant, calmly and matter-of-factly phrased interjections actually have a distancing effect on the readers' emotions towards Mary, and the rhetorical effect of the text is rational, rather than affective.

Beth Tobin has argued that nineteenth-century writers like Elizabeth Gaskell and Anne Bronte "sought to destabilize traditional moral authority and to erect in its place a new, feminine version of moral authority" based on "feminine traits such as sympathy and kindness" (Tobin 105), an argument that is obviously related to my own. She maintains that this feminine moral authority was the direct result of Hannah More's "professing a 'religion of the heart'. . . better suited to women and their newly constructed feminine graces of sympathy and kindness than to men" (Tobin 111). There is undoubted truth to Tobin's reasoning, but the fact remains that Hannah More's tracts are significantly different from sentimentalist texts because these narratives do not dramatize suffering but instead rely on logical argument in that the stories "prove" the truth of the lessons the author prescribes. More did not wish to over-arouse the emotions of her audience because she believed that over-arousal would lead to what she described in her tracts as the "wrong" kind of charity.

Another pamphlet from the *Cheap Repository Tracts*, "The Cottage Cook," presents the most evident example of More's aversion to excessive emotion. The opening of this text characterizes its heroine Mrs. Jones by her excessive feelings and her capacity to be easily moved. After the village rector preaches a moving sermon on charity one Sunday, he calls on Mrs. Jones and finds her "in tears" because, as he tells him, she has "been much *moved* by his discourse, and she wept because she had so little to give to the plate, for though she *felt* very keenly for the poor in these dear times, yet she could not assist them" (More, vol. 4, p.6, emphasis added).

This capacity to be moved by others' misfortunes seems to set Mrs. Jones up as a potentially good heroine for a sentimentalist social reform novel, in which her emotional responses would lead her not only to feel, but to do good things for those around her. More, however, presented emotion as an undesirable impediment, and her narrator interjects disapprovingly that "she [Mrs. Jones] was not aware how wrong it was to weep away that time which might have been better spent in drying the tears of others" (6). After inaugurating a new life of practical charity, Mrs. Jones never weeps again in "The Cottage Cook" or in the two sequel tracts that follow it. More also attacked generosity based on emotion in her tract "Estimate of the Religion of the Fashionable World" because for her, acts of charity based only on feeling, and not on a disciplined faith in God, were morally suspect (Tobin 96).

This attitude is demonstrated in "The Cottage Cook," because Mrs. Jones' new usefulness, resulting from the severity of the pastor, takes the form of her inducing various people to behave correctly, through logic and appeals to their self-interest. She convinces the two local gentlemen to donate money for building a large parish oven, and we are told that "Sir John subscribed to be rid of her importunity, and the squire because he thought every improvement in economy would reduce the poor-rate [tax used for poor relief]" (19). More's moral vision, as opposed to Tonna's, presumed the existence of a tightly-knit rural community in which all citizens, both rich and poor, were interdependent, and therefore supported each other because they had common interests. Also, Tonna's work was influenced by the increasingly fixed gender binaries prescribed by the domestic ideology, in which women's charitable acts were constructed as the result of their "naturally" more emotional and sympathetic temperaments, not of reason.

The results of the shifts in social structure described earlier in this chapter can be seen clearly in the transition from "The Lancashire Collier Girl" to *Helen Fleetwood*. It is Tonna who uses her culturally sanctioned role to bring the suffering of the workers and urban poor to the attention of her audience. The happy confidence with which More assumes that the problems of the poor can be solved with judicious, personalized charity like that of Mrs. Jones has been replaced by Tonna's strident outcries against the indifference of the middle and upper classes. More assumes the existence of the communal affective bonds that allow individualized charity to take place; Tonna must construct these bonds artificially through the power of her discourse and the cultural assumptions embedded in the domestic ideology: "The abstract idea of a suffering family does not strongly affect the mind; but let the parties be known to us, let their names call up some familiar images to our view, and . . . we are enabled much more feelingly to enter into their trial" (*The Wrongs of Woman* 120). It is in order to create these affective bonds that Tonna relies on the "feminine" language of sentiment and morality; changes in social and economic conditions have clearly resulted in a new, more strident and emotionally engaging, feminized discourse that would remind its audience of their responsibilities as Christians.

Research has suggested that there is a large body of social reform literature by women in the nineteenth century—literature that accompanied active female involvement in anti-slavery crusades, philanthropy, and support for foreign missions. These works of literature—ranging in political and religious orientation from Charlotte Elizabeth Tonna's strict Evangelicalism to Caroline Norton's airy Romanticism and Elizabeth Gaskell's liberal Unitarianism—all shared common characteristics. Whether they were novels, poems, or short stories, they held in common a willingness to use a morally urgent, rhetorical stance and a passionate emotionalism that attempted to move readers emotionally by creating a kind of rhetorical identification with suffering characters. With both of these sentimentalist techniques, these works took advantage of nineteenth-century constructions of womanhood by drawing on sentimental religious and 'family' values in order to get their points across.

For example, Caroline Norton's 1836 poem "A Voice From the Factories" counted on her audience's "native" pity (260) and their agreement that "Ever a toiling child make us sad/ . . . Because we feel their smiles should be so glad" (245). In the poem, Norton also maintained that a happy, innocent childhood is a God-given right—a substitute for the Paradise that we lost after the Fall. She condemned those whose "commercial avarice" (248) made them deny Christ's commands: "Nor should we, Christians in a Christian land,/ Forget who smiled on helpless infancy,/ And blessed them with a divinely gentle hand" (259). Although Caroline Norton and Charlotte Elizabeth Tonna moved in entirely different circles—Norton was a socialite who was later at the center of scandalous divorce case, whereas Tonna was a pious, Evangelical activist—Norton's techniques were very similar to Tonna's own manipulation of her audience's "natural" sympathy and their religious beliefs. For instance both Tonna and Norton used the same biblical passage (Matthew 19:13) in *The Wrongs of Woman* and "A Voice from the Factories," and like Tonna in both *Wrongs* and *Helen Fleetwood*, Norton asked her female readers to compare the child laborers to their own children.

Yet another female writer who was distinct from Tonna and Norton, yet used the same sentimentalist conventions, was

Frances Trollope. Although now known mainly as the mother of novelist Anthony Trollope, Frances Trollope was in 1839 a well-known writer in her own right, author of several novels and travel memoirs, including her celebrated and controversial *Domestic Manners of the Americans* (1832). In 1839, Trollope decided to write a novel "on the condition of the factory hands" (Heineman 169), anticipating the better known "Condition of England" novelists Elizabeth Gaskell, Benjamin Disraeli, Charles Kingsley, and Charles Dickens. While it could be that her initial decision was due more to market considerations than genuine conviction—she had already found with *Jonathan Jefferson Whitlaw*, an 1836 novel on American slavery, that topicality paid off—it is certain that Trollope approached the project seriously because she went to Manchester, toured the slums, visited several factories, and interviewed several Chartist leaders as preparation for writing the novel.

In *The Life and Adventures of Michael Armstrong, Factory Boy*, Michael gets "adopted" by a cruel and hypocritical factory owner, Sir Matthew Dowling, who is trying to impress people with his generosity and kindness. When Michael does not show his gratitude sufficiently because he is too loyal to his mother and crippled brother, Sir Matthew punishes Michael by indenturing him to the horrific Deep Valley Mill, where parish orphans labor in obscure, unseen misery. Meanwhile, a rich heiress, Mary Brotherton, decides to break out of her protected, privileged world by learning all she can about the despised laboring men, women, and children who make that world possible. Trollope uses Mary's interest in Michael to gradually arouse her middle- and upper-class audience's sympathies, as, interspersed with Michael's story, Mary's shocking discoveries stand in for the readers' own journey through Trollope's revelations.

Some have argued that *Michael Armstrong* is not a successful novel because the actual plot loses so much of its interest after Mary, having been misinformed that Michael is dead, takes Michael's orphaned friend, Fanny and his crippled brother Edward, to live with her abroad. Michael's own escape from Deep Valley Mill, his subsequent melodramatic adventures trying to find Fanny and Edward, and the unrealistic double wedding at the end pale in comparison to the obvious lack of resolution in the factories. Trollope moves her main characters to a sheltered life abroad, where they are insulated by Mary's money from any future involvement with the factory system.

It can be argued, however, that Trollope intended the novel's denouement to be improbable and shallow, as its emotional center is clearly its impassioned denunciation of the factory system's abuses: the bound edition's Preface announces that "it was her [Trollope's] intention . . . to drag into the light of day, and place before the eyes of Englishmen, the hideous mass of injustice and suffering to which thousands of infant labourers are subjected, who toil in our monster spinning mills" (*Michael Armstrong* iii). Accompanied by Auguste Hervieu's engravings, her detailed and graphic descriptions of suffering were powerful weapons against child labor:

> For who can think of villainous smells, or heed the suffering of the ear-racking sounds, while they look upon hundreds of helpless children, divested of every trace of health, of joyousness, and even of youth! (*Michael Armstrong* 80)

Trollope dealt not only with child labor in *Michael Armstrong*, but with all of the ramifications of it that would have shocked Victorian readers: parents exploiting their children's labor in order to live, the disintegration of poor families, and, more than anything else, the huge gulf between the laborers and the callous, pretentious lives of the manufacturers who profit from their workers' labor, while expressing contempt for them at the same time and turning them into a despised, isolated, underclass. Trollope theorized that this hypocrisy enabled the manufacturers to keep the truth a secret from the public, based on her premise that if English people actually knew about the evils inherent in the factory system, they would not tolerate it.

The real problem was, according to Trollope, that the facts were not presented to the public in the right way. As a humanitarian, activist clergyman says in the novel: "were a patient, accurate, and laborious detail of all the enormities committed, and all the sufferings endured, under the factory system, to be presented to the public, it would be thrown aside by some as greatly too tedious for belief" (202–3). The novel itself, therefore, tries to do what is lacking in its internal world—it becomes an advocate for the factory workers by dramatizing the issue in novel form, interspersed with occasional authorial reminders of the narrative's veracity:

> Let none dare to say this picture is exaggerated, til he has taken the trouble to ascertain by his own personal investigation, that it is so.... [W]oe to those who supinely sit in contented ignorance . . . while thousands of helpless children pine away their unnoted, miserable lives, in labour and destitution . . . (186)

The novel was not popular with some reviewers, ostensibly because of the "coarseness" of its subject matter: Trollope herself said, "I don't think that anyone cares much for *Michael Armstrong*—except the Chartists. A new kind of patrons for me!" (Heineman 171). Samuel Kydd's *History of the Factory Movement* (1857), however, commended Tonna's *Helen Fleetwood* and Frances Trollope's *Michael Armstrong, Factory Boy* among those works that helped the cause of factory reform (Cazamian 235). Their influence is confirmed by Louis Cazamian, who stated that the two novels "were successful and influential in their day" (235).

Most importantly, the parallels among Trollope, Tonna, and Norton indicate that this feminized sentimentalist discourse is common to many nineteenth-century women writers, crossing the lines of social class, and religious and political affiliations. While not all of these women would have agreed with each other—for instance, Elizabeth Stone, a native of Manchester, wrote *William Langshawe, the Cotton Lord* (1842) in order to dispute the portrayals of villainous factory owners in works like Tonna's *Helen Fleetwood* and Trollope's *Michael Armstrong, Factory Boy*—they had a common interest in advocating feminized social values as solutions for social problems.

These works are also impressive in the range of issues that they dealt with. In the early years of the nineteenth century, many British women were involved in the anti-slavery movement. Charlotte Elizabeth Tonna's first novel, *The System* (1827), was written during this period. Women writers also wrote works about the wrongs done to seamstresses: Julia Kavanagh's *Rachel Gray* (1856), Eliza Meteyard's *Lucy Dean: the Noble Needlewoman* (1850), Camilla Toulmin's *The Orphan Milliners: A Story of the West End* (1844), Charlotte Elizabeth Tonna's "The Lace-Runners" from *The Wrongs of Woman*, Frances Trollope's *Jessie Philips* (1844), and Elizabeth Stone's *The Young Milliner* (1843). As I have shown, they wrote novels, stories, and poems about the problems created by industrialism: in addition to the authors and works I discussed in this chapter (Tonna, Norton, and Trollope), there are several others, such as: Caroline Bowles' "Tales of the Factories" (1833), Elizabeth Barrett Browning's "Cry of the Children" (1844), Fanny Mayne's *Jane Rutherford; or the Miner's Strike* (1853), Elizabeth Stone's *William Langshawe, the Cotton Lord* (1842), Geraldine Jewsbury's *Marian Withers* (1851). Finally, of course, there are the works of Elizabeth Gaskell, *Mary Barton* and *North and South*, which I will discuss at greater length in the fourth chapter of this book. With the exception of those by Gaskell and Elizabeth Barrett Browning, none of these works are currently in print, and one of my goals in this study is to rectify this situation by explaining why these writers deserve to be read and studied.

In 1977, the feminist writer Ellen Moers wrote about Charlotte Elizabeth Tonna: "Of all the minor women of the epic age, this lady . . . Mrs. Tonna . . . is the one about whom I most wish to satisfy my curiosity" (Moers 36). Moer's curiosity was certainly warranted, as Charlotte Elizabeth Tonna's long and distinguished writing career would certainly seem to merit more recognition than it has received. In the years since Moer's statement, Tonna's life and work have achieved some recognition from such critics as Joseph Kestner, Ivanka Kovacevic and Barbara Kanner, Catherine Gallagher, and Christine Krueger. All of these critics recognize Tonna's importance as part of the historical record; Joseph Kestner argues, for example, that *The Wrongs of Woman* is "an important text of social industrial protest" (Kestner 212). Although Kestner closes his essay with the statement that "the nineteenth-century canon must be expanded to include such achievements," he fails to explain or theorize why a text that he analyzes, in effect, as a historical document should even be considered as literature (212). Kestner inherits this problem from other critical considerations of Tonna's work—for instance, Barbara Kanner and Ivanka Kovacevic, who, again, put up a spirited defense of Tonna's historical importance, while stating flatly that "the literary value of her [Tonna's] writing is too mediocre to call for defense" (158). As I argued in the previous chapter, however, such assessments depend on a modernist definition of literature that is outdated, narrow, and a-historical, and that this definition obviously must be questioned if the contributions of writers like Tonna are to be recognized and appreciated on their own literary merits. Tonna's *Helen Fleetwood*, for example, is well-plotted and moving—the novel's central situation, that of the Green family's being forced to move to Manchester, is realistic, and the important scenes, such as Mrs. Green's failure to get help from the factory owner Mr. Z, are spare, simple, and effective.[21] Frances Trollope's *Michael Armstrong*, on the other hand, makes expert use of satire and humor: her descriptions of Dowling Lodge and its master and mistress as an example of the new-monied lifestyle created by industrialism are satirical caricatures fully as effective as any produced by Dickens.

Furthermore, in addition to their own merits, these sentimentalist women writers also, obviously, have an enormous cultural significance, both in terms of their historical impact and through their influence on other writers. Specifically, the sentimentalist cultural discourse of social reform, dominated by these women writers, set the tone and parameters of the entire discourse of social reform in the Victorian period. Thereafter, no social reform writer, whether liberal or conservative, male or female, could afford to ignore the power of sentimentalist conventions in directing public opinion. Later on in this book, I will discuss this issue at length in relation to Elizabeth Gaskell and will also suggest its significance for our understanding of other women writers, such as Elizabeth Barrett Browning. My first task, however, is to show how sentimentalist discourse had a crucial impact on the literary production and reception of one figure whose status in the canon has never been seriously

---

[21] I discuss Mrs. Green's quest for assistance from Mr. Z at greater length in the fourth chapter of this book.

threatened: Charles Dickens. Dickens' work, with its extensive use of pathos, its preachiness, and its references to biblical eschatology, shares many features in common with, and indeed can be considered a part of, sentimentalist discourse. I have always agreed with Raymond Williams' conclusion that Dickens' fiction advocates the creation of moral consciousness, and it is clear that this goal, and many of the techniques that Dickens used to achieve it, come from the influence of sentimentalism, a feminized discourse whose lowly features have been scorned by generations of literary critics.

Chapter Three

"Mr. Popular Sentiment": Dickens and the Gender Politics of Sentimentalist Discourse

The career of Charles Dickens is a crucial site for investigating the gender politics of sentimentalist social reform discourse because in order to be effective as a social reform writer who opposed the masculinized discourses of Utilitarianism and laissez-faire capitalism, Dickens used the same feminized language of emotion and sentiment associated with women writers. When he said in an 1854 article opposing the ideas of political economy that "into the relations between employers and employed . . . there must enter something of feeling and sentiment" ("On Strike" 553), Dickens echoed the ideas and the language of cultural agents like the 1853 *Gentleman's Magazine* review I discussed in the previous chapter: "our literature and our morals require more and more for their basis a sound increasing knowledge and sympathy between all orders of men . . . [which] women can especially forward" ("Lady Novelists of Great Britain" 24). Statements like the one in the *Gentleman's Magazine* review, however, identified women, with their "naturally" more emotional and sympathetic perspective, as ideal social reform writers, and the Victorian reading public seems to have concurred with this identification, as feminist critic Christine Krueger has pointed out: "By 1850 the tradition of the woman preacher as the writer of the social narrative had been thoroughly integrated into Victorian culture. Women were expected to place their literary talents in the service of social reform" (231).

As Krueger suggests, these cultural expectations affected women writers, because while on one hand writers like Elizabeth Gaskell were given a powerful political voice through their social reform writing, this writing was limited in both tone and subject matter. But Dickens' own position as a male writer trying to work within this feminized discourse was also fraught with difficulty, both within the Victorian period and in his critical history since.

Like Charlotte Elizabeth Tonna, Dickens used fiction to advocate the creation of moral consciousness; he played the role of the "good spirit who would take the house-tops off. . . and show a Christian people. . . pale phantoms rising from the scenes of our too-long neglect" (*Dombey and Son* 738). Sentimentalist social reform discourse, with its use of Christian preaching and pathetic scenes of physical and emotional suffering, was clearly one of the most effective methods that he used to fulfill that design. The "exaggerated forms" of Dickens' characters—such as the crossing-sweeper Jo in *Bleak House* and Betty Higden in *Our Mutual Friend*—enabled his readers to see and feel the urban poor, even as Tonna's readers saw and felt the workers in the textile mills (*Critical Heritage* 524). In other words, Dickens' fiction often had the same moralistic sense of social purpose, and reliance on pathos and emotionalism, that his audience normally associated with women writers. If we lay out some key Victorian cultural assumptions in a series of binaries that have been suggested by Nancy Armstrong, Jane Tompkins, and other feminist critics, it is possible to see that Dickens fits in the right-hand column of all of the binary pairs except, conspicuously, the first:

male	female
intellect/mind	emotion/heart
objectivity	sympathy
abstract	personalized
financial/physical power	spiritual/moral power
realistic/objective	sentimental

Although these binaries essentialize gender, I think that feminist critics such as Nancy Armstrong have already demonstrated their cultural significance for the production and reception of women's writing in the nineteenth century. What I want to do is demonstrate their cultural significance for the production and reception of Dickens' writing.

I contend that Dickens' "cross-dressing"—the disjunction between Dickens' own gender and the "gender" of his fiction—has, in many ways, shaped both Dickens' work and its critical reception over the years. On one hand, Dickens' admirers, such as Queen Victoria, praised Dickens' "large loving mind and . . . strongest sympathy with the poorer classes," domesticized feminine virtues which made his death "a great loss"(*Critical Heritage* 502).[1] On the other hand, many critics also agreed with Thomas Carlyle's assessment that, like a woman (or, more accurately, like the nineteenth-century idea of the domesticized woman), Dickens based his ideas about social issues on his emotional reactions and was simply incapable of grappling intellectually with complex social problems—which meant that he wasn't taken seriously as an artist or a social critic.[2] Intellectuals, both in the nineteenth century and later, came to look down on Dickens' lack of formal education and his engagement with popular culture; he was considered by George Henry Lewes to be "completely outside philosophy, science, and the higher literature"

---

[1] In his funeral sermon for Dickens, Dean Arthur Stanley also celebrated Dickens' efforts to create connections between social classes:

> By him that veil was rent asunder which parts the various classes of society. Through his genius the rich man . . . was made to see and feel the presence of the Lazarus at his gate. The unhappy inmates of the workhouse, the neglected children in the dens and caves of our great cities...far from the observation of men...had been, it may be sometimes, in exaggerated forms, made to stand and speak before those who hardly dreamed of their existence. (Collins, *Dickens: the Critical Heritage* 524)

Stanley's construction of Dickens credits Dickens' fiction with creating affective bonds between classes and assigns Dickens the role of preacher—a role held in common with women writers like Charlotte Elizabeth Tonna who, in the words of Christine Krueger, were thought to be the "evangelists of reconciliation" (157).

[2] Carlyle saw Dickens as a "good little fellow" with one of the most "cheery, innocent natures he had ever encountered," but thought that Dickens' "theory of life was entirely wrong" because it was too "soft and accomodating" (Collins, *Dickens: Interviews and Recollections* 63).

(*Dickens: Interviews and Recollections* 26) and by Victorian literary critic, Fitzjames Stephen, to be "utterly destitute of any kind of solid acquirements" (Stephen 9).[3] The identification of "Mr. Popular Sentiment" (as Anthony Trollope labelled Dickens in his 1855 novel, *The Warden*) with sentiment and sympathy, and with popular culture, aligned him with nineteenth-century cultural constructions of femininity; indeed, Fitzjames Stephen said that Dickens' "melodramatic and sentimental stock-in-trade" was well suited to "a feminine, irritable, noisy mind, which is always clamouring and shrieking for guidance" (Stephen 9).[4]

This wide divergence in response can be partially explained by shifts in critical values that occurred in the nineteenth century, as the Romantic idealism of the early nineteenth century gave way to Realism and then to Aestheticism. In the eighteen-thirties and

---

[3] I agree with Harold Orel that Lewes, unlike Fitzjames Stephen, did not consider himself one of the critics who wrote about Dickens with "mingled irritation and contempt," and he did concede Dickens' "glorious energy of imagination" (Lewes, *Literary Criticism*, 99 and 97). In the final analysis, however, Lewes' assessment of Dickens, the essay "Dickens in Relation to Criticism" in *The Fortnightly Review*, 1872, is more about Dickens' deficiencies than it is his strengths. I cannot disagree with George Ford's immortal characterization of Lewes' attitude towards Dickens:

> His [Lewes'] expression throughout his essay is as if a bad smell had penetrated into his library. He has gone out to the kitchen to find out what the help have been eating with such enthusiasm, and he has brought back a plateful to his desk for examination and analysis. His own sniff of disapproval is unrelieved, though he does take pains to explain why the kitchen help are under the illusion that the dish is tasty. (Ford 151)

[4] Stephen's use of the indefinite article makes it unclear whether he meant to accuse Dickens himself or Dickens' reading public of having "a feminine, irritable, and noisy mind;" either way, however, the statement links Dickens with femininity in a far from complimentary manner.

forties Francis Jeffrey, the "hanging judge" of literary critics during the Romantic period, wept openly on reading Dickens' famous deathbed scenes in *The Old Curiosity Shop* and *Dombey and Son*, and his Christmas Books,[5] but by the eighteen-sixties and seventies critics like Lewes and Stephen were openly disparaging Dickens' sentimentality even though his popularity with the reading public remained relatively unaffected.

In an 1899 critical study, *The Development of the English Novel*, the Yale scholar, Wilbur Cross, theorized that:

> The effect of Dickens's pathos has, in the lapse of a half-century, undergone change; it seems to be of a fanciful world far removed from the actual. It no longer moves to tears, but awakens rather a pleasing aesthetic emotion, because of its poetic qualities, most completely manifest in the marvellous description of Paul Dombey's death. . . . The time comes when both the public and the critic express their want of sympathy with all premeditated emotion by calling it sentimentalism. Against the current offhand condemnation of Dickens's sentimentalism history, however, will surely protest . . . (186)

The contrast between the comments of Jeffrey and Cross effectively demonstrates the critical turn away from sentimentalism. By the eighteen-nineties, Cross, in response to

---

[5]In a letter to Dickens responding to *The Chimes* (1844), Jeffrey wrote:

> Blessings on your kind heart, my dearest Dickens, for *that*, after all, is your great talisman, and the gift for which you will be not only most loved, but longest remembered. Your kind and courageous advocacy of the rights of the poor . . . have done more to soothe desponding worth—to waken sleeping (almost dead) humanities—and to shame even selfish brutality, than all the other writings of the age, and make it, and all that are to come after, your debtors.
>
> You understand from this . . . that the music of your chimes [has] reached me, and resounded through my heart, and that I thank you with all that is left of it.
>
> . . . but I could not *reserve* my tears for your third part. From the meeting with Will on the street, they flowed and ebbed at your bidding; and I know you will forgive me for saying that my interest in the story began there. (Cockburn 390-1)

famous dismissals like Oscar Wilde's statement that "one must have a heart of stone to read the death of Little Nell without laughing" (Ellman 469), must present an apologia for Dickens' use of pathos. Finally, in an age dominated by New Criticism, it is probably no accident that Dickens, "the thorn in the flesh [of] the formalist" (Edgar 122), reached the nadir of his critical reputation. Pelham Edgar's 1934 "systematic study of the structural evolution of the English novel" is a good example of the typical formalist/ structuralist dismissal of Dickens. Dickens, according to Edgar, was "one of the anomalies of literature who would seem to have produced a great result by defective means" and was a "standing menace to the academic critic" (117). In contrast to Dickens, Edgar argued that "[George] Eliot and Hardy hold secure rank as thinkers" (151). Edgar chiefly disliked Dickens' sensationalism, including his sentimentality, and the moralizing commentary, which was the result of Dickens' unfortunate "view that the novel was an instrument of social regeneration" (123). This criticism illustrates the final turn against the feminized values of sentimentalism; as Suzanne Clark has argued, "The modernist new critics used aesthetic anti-sentimentality . . . to establish a position against mass culture. Mass culture was a feminized enemy they saw as dangerous" (5).

Most importantly, however, all of these critical assessments implicitly show how Dickens was aligned with the "feminine" side of the gender binaries, both before and after the shift in critical values. The alignment had advantages, as Dickens was celebrated for his "goodness" and "kindly feelings,"[6] but it also hindered his capacity to be taken seriously as an intellectual or an artist, even during his lifetime. This dilemma, I believe, provides valuable insights into Dickens' career as a novelist and social reformer and his relationships with his female colleagues. Dickens' novels

---

[6]These words are taken from Jeffrey's letter complimenting Dickens on *A Christmas Carol*, Dec. 8, 1843 (Cockburn 380–1). It is interesting to note that both Cross and Edgar, while noting Dickens' formal defects, still express admiration for Dickens' "finer qualities" of heart (Edgar 117).

contain many elements in common with sentimentalist discourse: his use of pathos, his narrative "preachiness," the way that he alluded to commonly-held religious beliefs in order to support his views. Moreover, he publicly supported many of the same causes as crusading women reformers like Tonna: causes such as factory reform, poor relief, the reclamation of prostitutes, etc. Even while he favored these causes, however, he continually distanced himself from sentimentalist female social reformers, and even satirized them in caricatures such as Mrs. Jellyby and Mrs. Pardiggle in *Bleak House*. In the first part of the chapter, I will read one of Dickens' earliest novels, *Oliver Twist*, as an example of sentimentalist cultural discourse, and show how the gender binaries in the novel play an important part in the novel's cultural work. Secondly, I will analyze Dickens' relationships with his female colleagues, also social reform writers, in order to demonstrate how his uneasy alignment with sentimentalist discourse affected his concept of himself as an artist. Even while writing sentimentalist fiction himself, Dickens tried to claim artistic superiority over women sentimentalist writers, like Frances Trollope and Harriet Beecher Stowe, by constructing them as imitators of his own works.

I. "My glance at the New Poor Law:" Pathos and Parish Boys in *Oliver Twist*

Oliver Twist was the first Dickens novel that Dickens himself planned from beginning to end, since the original idea of *Pickwick Papers* had come from its publishers, Chapman and Hall. He wrote that he had "thrown his whole heart and soul" into it and it is evident that the criticism of the New Poor Law was a key element in his design from the very beginning (*Letters*, vol. 1, 227).[7] The philosophy of the Whig-sponsored New Poor Law, passed in

---

[7]In a letter to his friend Thomas Beard the Saturday before the publication of the *Bentley's Miscellany* containing the opening installment of *Oliver Twist*, Dickens called it "my glance at the new poor Law Bill" (*Letters*, vol. 1, 231).

1834, was based on Utilitarian theories of political economy modified by Malthusian theories of population.[8] Designed to discourage pauperism, it changed the old model of parish poor relief (still basically derived from the old Elizabethan Poor Law) into a more centralized system that established workhouses for the ablebodied poor and forbade parishes to offer free relief for those able to work. Following the classic theories of economists, the law discouraged freeloaders by making workhouse life deliberately less attractive than private employment. Inmates were kept on a deliberately sparse diet, denied outdoor exercise, received poor medical care, and married couples were separated so that they could not produce children to further burden the parish.[9] The Utilitarians who originated and supported the law probably intended for it to be more humanely enforced, and resented what they saw as a cheap emotional attack based on ignorance—an accusation that reinforced Dickens' feminized cultural position. Dickens' opposition constructed him as a well-meaning, but basically ignorant, individual who was too easily moved by pathos and was misleading society by his sentimental and hysterical rhetoric.

Harriet Martineau, a well-known public defender of political economy, made this somewhat restrained comment on this subject in her *Autobiography*, deploring Dickens' "vigorous erroneousness about matters of science, as shown in *Oliver Twist* about the new

---

[8]Conservative historian Gertrude Himmelfarb argues in *The Idea of Poverty* (1984) that "it was under the aegis of Malthus and Ridardo that political economy freed itself from its ties to moral philosophy . . . . This "naturalization" of economics had momentous consequences for society as a whole, and for the poor in particular. For it threatened to undermine whatever remained of the 'moral economy'. . . " (101).

[9]E. P. Thompson argues in *The Making of the English Working Class* that the poor law was "perhaps the most sustained attempt to impose an ideological dogma, in defiance of the evidence of human need, in English history" (267), a conclusion with which Dickens probably would have agreed—as *Oliver Twist* shows.

poor-law . . . . [T]here are many who wish that he [Dickens] would abstain from a set of difficult subjects, on which all true sentiment must be underlain by a sort of knowledge which he has not. The more fervent and inexhaustible his kindliness (and it is fervent and inexhaustible) the more important it is that it should be well-informed . . ." (*Autobiography*, vol. 2, 62).[10] This critique responds to Dickens' own use of the feminized cultural values of sentimentalist social reform discourse in *Oliver Twist*. The way that Dickens connects evil and cruelty with a cold and ruthlessly self-serving Utilitarian "philosophy" sets up two entirely opposed value systems in the novel, a "masculine" Utilitarian value system and a feminine one based on sentimental morality, and these two competing value systems make the novel itself a site of competing discourses. In addition, although the novel heavily favors the sentimental value system as the only available option in opposition to the Utilitarian values represented by the New Poor Law and Fagin's gang, it also betrays Dickens' discomfort with the gender binaries that classify these value systems. This discomfort, I believe, is emblematic of Dickens own vexed position as a male sentimentalist.

The "good" characters in *Oliver Twist*, such as Mr. Brownlow and the Maylies, are explicitly shown to base their actions on altruistic impulses that derive from sympathetic feelings, and these characters are feminized as a result. Almost all of Mr. Brownlow's actions in the novel come from strong feelings, from his behavior at Oliver's trial to his final confrontations with Monks and Fagin, and these feelings usually manifest themselves

---

[10]In an 1855 pamphlet, "The Factory Controversy: A Warning Against Meddling Legislation" (written around the same time as her *Autobiography*), Martineau again attacked the interventionist views of Dickens and other humanitarians as "the pseudo-philanthropy which is one of the disgraces of our times" (95). She also criticized Dickens specifically, as having "acted the part of sentimental philanthropist in *Oliver Twist*" (95) and demanded that Dickens' audience " require from him some soundness of principle and some depth of knowledge . . ." (96).

in feminized physical reactions, including those associated with sentimentality. The sight of Oliver recovering from his illness, for example, moves him to stereotypically sentimental tears: "Mr. Brownlow's heart, being large enough for any six ordinary old gentlemen of humane disposition, forced a supply of tears into his eyes, by some hydraulic process which we are not sufficiently philosophical to be in a condition to explain" (129–30). The sarcasm in this passage places Brownlow's display of feeling in explicit opposition to the "philosophical" (Utilitarian) failure to account for feeling; his tears are the outward signs of a "heart" that is somehow outside the understanding of masculine discourses like philosophy or science. Brownlow's actions in this scene in fact echo those of a specific woman, his old housekeeper Mrs. Bedwin, who begins "to cry most violently" because of her "considerable delight at seeing him [Oliver] so much better" (128). Like Dickens, Mrs. Bedwin also asserts the "normality" of these emotional tears, assuring Oliver that "I'm only having a good cry . . . and I'm quite comfortable" (128). Oliver's other benefactors, the Maylies, are also prone to these displays of feeling, which are endorsed and even added to by the novel's narrative commentary, especially in the scenes of Rose Maylie's illness and near escape from death.[11]

---

[11] Angus Wilson, in his introduction to the Penguin edition of *Oliver Twist*, says that these scenes directly reflect "his [Dickens'] powerful feelings about the sudden death of his seventeen-year-old sister in law, Mary Hogarth." Wilson argues that "the effect upon Dickens' artistry of this powerful personal sentiment is disastrous. It causes him to invent a whole mawkish episode in which Rose almost dies . . . it leads him to describe her in language artificial and inept" (20). Although Wilson is most likely correct in arguing that Mary Hogarth's death probably did influence Dickens' portrayal of Rose's illness, he fails to contextualize this episode within the way that the whole novel relies on a sentimentalist understanding of emotion, and on a sentimentalist understanding of death.

In fact, it is in its treatment of death that this novel, and Dickens' other novels, most resembles sentimentalist discourse. As Jane Tompkins has pointed out, death scenes in sentimentalist discourse are of supreme cultural importance because they use commonly held religious beliefs in order to judge the injustices of the world by a higher, heavenly standard. When Stowe's Little Eva, passing from life into death, exclaims "O love!—joy!—peace!" (Stowe 428), she "testifies to the reality of the life to come" and to all that that entails (Tompkins 129). According to the system of eschatological Christian beliefs that guides this vision, the earthly world is subject to the cosmic order of a higher power, and the deaths of characters like Little Dick in *Oliver Twist* and Jo in *Bleak House* serve to remind both the other characters and the audience of that order. When Oliver says goodbye to Dick before travelling to London, for example, Dick already prefigures his own death and "testifies to the reality of the life to come' (Tompkins 129): "'I heard the doctor say I was dying,' replied the child with a faint smile,. . . 'I know the doctor must be right, Oliver, because I dream so much of Heaven, and Angels, and kind faces that I never see when I am awake'" (96). Moreover, many of Dickens' other novels make use of the sentimentalist understanding of death, especially (but not limited to) the deaths of children: to name a few, the deaths of Little Nell in *The Old Curiousity Shop*, Little Paul Dombey in *Dombey and Son*, Smike in *Nicholas Nickleby*, William and Frederick Dorrit in *Little Dorrit*, and baby Johnny in *Our Mutual Friend*. The sentimentalist value system also informs that quintessentially Dickensian text, *A Christmas Carol*, since it is, finally, Scrooge's encounters with the possible death of Tiny Tim, and with his own death in the person of the Spirit of Christmas Yet To Come, that lead to his becoming a more generous and sympathetic individual.

These sentimental religious values, which characterize so much of Dickens' fiction, have been summarily dismissed by critics because they have been interpreted as "repositories of cliches from which to draw to evoke automatic reactions for certain kinds of novelistic occasions, such as the child's deathbed or the exaltation of the heroine's virtues" (Larson 6). The "cliché" of the child's deathbed, however, is one of the many aspects of Dickens' work that can be better understood in the context of sentimentalist discourse. The weepy, sentimentalist understanding of death, as embodied by Little Dick and other scenes in *Oliver Twist*, is a crucial part of the sentimental value system that Dickens proposes in opposition to a "masculine," self-serving Utilitarianism which attempts to crush sympathy and sentiment in the name of "philosophical" self-interest.

The values of the "evil" characters, both the parish officials who exploit and mistreat Oliver in the beginning of the novel and the members of the criminal underworld represented by Fagin and his gang, are based on these "masculine," self-serving theories of Utilitarian political economy. In *Oliver Twist*, Dickens portrays the Poor Law's wrongs as directly resulting from its "philosophy" of emotionless practicality. He calls the appropriately named Mrs. Mann, the woman who runs the branch-workhouse where Oliver spends his early childhood, a "very great experimental philosopher" because acting on her "accurate perception of what was good for herself" she "appropriated the greater part of the weekly stipend for her own use" (48). Similarly, the respectable members of the parish poor relief board are "sage, deep, philosophical men" because "they established the rule, that all poor people should have the alternative . . . of being starved by a gradual process in the house, or by a quick one out of it" (55). In order to reinforce what he believes is the evil nature of this Utilitarian philosophy Dickens also tries to rip off its mask of respectability by also describing the behavior of Fagin's gang of criminals in terms of "philosophy." When the Artful Dodger and Charley Bates allow the innocent Oliver to be arrested for their crime, for example, they show a "laudable and becoming regard for themselves" that "corroborate[s] and confirm[s] the little code of laws which certain profound and sound-judging philosophers have laid down as the mainsprings of all Nature's deeds and actions" (132).[12]

---

[12]K. J. Fielding follows a similar line of reasoning in a 1987 article on Utilitarianism and *Oliver Twist*. He argues that the novel

Neither Mrs. Mann nor the board members show sympathetic feelings towards Oliver, or towards anyone else for that matter, unless it is their practical interest to do so. The same goes for the parish beadle, Mr. Bumble, who only shows emotion when expedient, such as when he courts the well-left widow, Mrs. Corney, and believes that everyone else he encounters is equally insincere. When Oliver shows "horror and fear, too palpable to be mistaken" at the prospect of being indentured to a brutal chimney sweep and pleads for a magistrate's mercy, Bumble calls him an "artful and designing orphan" (65–66). And, although the respectable Mr. Bumble would be horrified at the very idea, Fagin and the other criminals reveal an attitude towards emotion similar to his, in the scene where Fagin and Bill Sikes rehearse Nancy for her mission to recover Oliver from the police after his arrest for pickpocketing:

> "Oh, my . . . poor, dear, sweet, innocent little brother!" exclaimed Miss Nancy, bursting into tears, and wringing the little basket and the street-door key in an agony of distress. "What has become of him!" . . . . Having uttered these words in a most lamentable and heartbroken tone to the immeasurable delight of her hearers, Miss Nancy paused, winked to the company, nodded smilingly round, and disappeared. (139–40)

Bumble, Fagin, and their ilk tend to see emotions, especially sympathetic emotions such as affection and grief, as strategies to be simulated in pursuit of ruthlessly businesslike goals.

So much so, in fact, that they fail to recognize real feeling when it presents itself to them. As when Bumble cannot see Oliver's fear and horror in the passage cited earlier, Fagin also fails to recognize Nancy's growing sympathy for Oliver. When she first intercedes to

---

connects the mistreatment of Oliver, both by the parish and by Fagin's gang, to Benthamite Utilitarian philosophy. Fielding's article only documents that connection in a direct comparison of *Oliver Twist* and Bentham's *Decontology*, however; he does not anticipate my description of the gendered nature of these polarized value systems in the novel, or discuss Dickens' use of genuine feeling, as a marker of positive social values.

protect the boy, he compliments her acting "more clever than ever tonight. Ha! ha! my dear, you are acting beautifully" (166) and is unpleasantly surprised by the reality of her "strong passions" (166), which increasingly ally her with the forces of good in the novel.

Dickens explicitly associates these feelings with Nancy's feminity—"There is something about a roused woman . . . which few men like to provoke" (166)—and this association suggests that, in the value system of *Oliver Twist*, there is something essentially feminine about Nancy's growing sympathy for Oliver, signified by her passionate emotional reactions, and her inability to stand seeing him mistreated. Fagin himself identifies Nancy's more sympathetic attitude towards Oliver as something in the nature of an occupational hazard: "It's the worst of having to do with women . . . but they're clever, and we can't get on, in our line, without 'em" (167). Moreover, Nancy's feminine sympathy, "the womanly feeling which she thought a weakness," debased after years on the streets as a prostitute, gets even more re-awakened by association with the stereotypically "feminine" Rose Maylie (361). Dickens' characterization of Rose identifies her, on the most literal level with the ideal sentimentalist heroine, the "Angel in the House": "The younger lady [Rose] was in the lovely bloom and spring-time of womanhood; at the age, when, if angels ever for God's good purposes enthroned in mortal forms, they may be, without impiety, supposed to abide in hers" (264). Nancy's "change of heart," her growing willingness to sacrifice herself for others, is strengthened by her association with Rose—this connection is symbolized by Nancy's clutching Rose's handkerchief as a talisman, almost as a holy relic, during Bill Sikes' final, murderous attack.[13] In addition, Dickens' naming of

---

[13]"She [Nancy] staggered and fell: nearly blinded with the blood that rained down from a deep gash in her forehead; but raising herself with difficulty, on her knees, drew from her bosom a white handkerchief—Rose Maylie's own—and holding it up, in her folded hands, as high towards Heaven as her feeble strength would allow, breathed one prayer for mercy to her Maker" (423).

the baby-farming Mrs. Mann also demonstrates how he aligns feminine feelings with goodness: since Mrs. Mann's actions are self-serving and reasonable, rather than altruistic and emotional, Dickens claims that she is, in effect, a man.[14]

This connection of goodness with feminized displays of feeling accounts for Dickens' "mawkish" and sentimental treatment of the good characters (Wilson 20). Conversely, what marks the evil characters in this novel is their failure to respond to occasions for sentimentality, like deathbeds, with the "change of heart" that is just as crucial to Dickens as it is to any other sentimentalist writer. Mr. Bumble and Mrs. Mann, for example, fail completely to appreciate the suffering of Little Dick: when Dick says that he will be "glad to die" and go to heaven, the two react with disbelief and cynicism: "I never see [sic] such a hard-hearted little wretch!" (173). Under the lens of a sentimentalist discourse of social reform, the sentimentality that most critics have seen as a flaw therefore reveals itself as an important aspect of the novel's design because in Dickens' construction of things, positive social values derive from feminized displays of genuine emotion. This construction links Dickens with the sentimentalist cultural discourse described in the previous chapter, a discourse primarily associated with feminized social values and with women writers.

The central figure of this novel, however, is not a woman but a boy—a boy, moreover, who continually exhibits "feminine" displays of feeling such as weeping, heart palpitating, and fainting because, as Dickens tells us early in the novel, "Oliver, instead of possessing too little feeling, possessed rather too much" (72). These characteristics, associated with sentimentalism, ensure Oliver's salvation, in one scene after another in the novel. Even in the beginning, Oliver escapes from indenture to the brutal chimney sweep by the open display of emotion before the magistrate that is looked on so suspiciously by Mr. Bumble, "He [Oliver] trembled violently, and burst into tears" (66). When first rescued from Fagin's gang by the intervention of Mr. Brownlow, Oliver (quite

---

[14]I would like to thank my colleague Dr. Holly McSpadden for pointing out the significance of Mrs. Mann's name to me.

unintentionally) convinces Mr. Brownlow and Mrs. Bedwin of his sensitivity and essential goodness with the way that he shows his strong emotions: he faints at the sight of the portrait of a dead woman who strongly resembles him (his mother, as it later turns out), and cries when he starts to tell Mr. Brownlow his life story. It is Oliver's "appearance and manner" (149) which arouse the sympathies of Brownlow and Mrs. Bedwin, and the same holds true later in the novel when Rose and Mrs. Maylie are moved by Oliver's attempts to "say . . . in a few tearful words, how deeply he felt the goodness of the two sweet ladies" (284–5). In the moral world of this novel, it seems to be better to have too much feeling than to have too little.

One cannot help noting, however, that it is this same quality of "too much feeling" that sets Oliver up to be a victim in one incident after another—at the hands of Mr. Bumble, Noah Claypole, the Artful Dodger, Fagin, and Bill Sikes. Moreover, Oliver is not the only one of Dickens' many heroes to suffer from the handicap of having "too much feeling." Compare Oliver, for example, to the young David Copperfield, who is given the girlish nickname "Daisy" by Steerforth. The "femininity" of Dickens' heroes was also noted by some astute contemporary readers of Dickens, such as Margaret Oliphant, who noted that "Their courage is of the order of courage which belongs to women" (Oliphant 451). These incidents seem to signify the instability of the gender binaries embedded in the Victorian domestic ideology, because if physical displays of emotion, and more highly developed moral sensibilities were to be associated mainly with women, as the domestic ideology dictated, then what becomes of the male sentimentalist? In fact, Oliver Twist's situation may be in many ways emblematic of Dickens' own dilemma as a male writer uneasily aligned with a feminized, sentimentalist social reform discourse.

II. "Sentimental Philanthropist," "Humanity-Monger," and "Feminine" Genius: the Struggles of a Literary Cross-Dresser

At at least two different points in his career, Dickens privately accused women writers of plagiarizing his ideas and fictional techniques, usually in snide "asides" written in letters to friends. These episodes, like the satire of women social reformers such as Mrs. Jellyby and Mrs. Pardiggle in his later novels, may have been signs of Dickens' efforts to fight the Victorian cultural imperatives that placed him in a feminized cultural space due to his use of feminized, sentimentalist techniques. The plagiarism episodes suggest, specifically, that Dickens used the legitimizing argument of artistic originality in order to claim himself as the "owner" of that cultural space and thereby exclude the female social reform writers who shared it with him by discrediting them.

In 1839, early in Dickens' career, Frances Trollope's novel, *Michael Armstrong, Factory Boy*, was published serially by Henry Colburn and advertised in the March, 1839 number of *Nicholas Nickleby* as "printed and embellished uniformly with the 'Pickwick Papers,' 'Nicholas Nickleby,' &c" (*Letters*, vol. 1, 506). This advertisement implied that Mrs. Trollope's novel was of the same type—in both senses of the word—as Dickens' novels, and set up comparisons between them which irritated him immensely.[15] Although Dickens protested that the comparisons between *Michael Armstrong* and his own works did not bother him, telling his informant Samuel Laman Blanchard on February 9, 1839 that "[i]f Mrs. Trollope were even to adopt Ticholas Tickleby as . . . a better sounding name than Michael Armstrong, I don't think it would cost me a wink of sleep, or impair my appetite in the smallest

---

[15]Dickens at this time had just finished running *Oliver Twist* in *Bentley's Miscellany*. He was writing *Nicholas Nickleby* serially for Chapman and Hall, and the advertisement for *Michael Armstrong* appeared in March monthly number of *Nicholas Nickleby*.

degree," his reaction to the advertisement shows to the contrary (*Letters*, vol. 1, 507).[16]

On February 8, 1839, the day that Dickens saw the advertisement for *Michael Armstrong*, sent to him by Blanchard, he wrote in his diary:

> Letter from Blanchard in the evening, inclosing another from Colburn relative to the Trollope advertisement, and its doubtfully honest or respectable imitation of Nickleby, which it seems was 'unintentional'—of course. Colburn himself called late at night but I was not visible. If they hurt anybody it will be themselves most likely—not me. (*Letters*, vol. 1, 640)

This entry is unusual, for most of Dicken's diary entries during this period simply record appointments, and are extremely brief, even perfunctory, and usually do not mention dealings with other writers. Dickens was upset enough, obviously, to alienate Colburn by refusing to see him—an impolitic and risky move for a young writer, even one as famous as Dickens already was—and the tone for the whole entry is rather sullen and defensive. Dickens' two letters to Blanchard also carry much the same tone, particularly when he stooped to insulting the Trollopes personally, "I will express no further opinion of Mrs. Trollope, than that I think *Mr.* Trollope must have been an old dog and chosen his wife from the same species," a remark that was even more inappropriate when made to someone like Blanchard, who was not a very close friend of Dickens' (*Letters*, vol. 1, 507).

It is true that this whole episode took place at a time when Dickens was particularly sensitive to the issue of copyright, and his concerns in this area are well documented. The best known of Dickens' imitators was an author published by Edward Lloyd who, under the pseudonym "Bos," produced a *Posthumorous Notes of the Pickwick Club*, an *Oliver Twiss*, and, in spite of Dickens' efforts with the public statement, a *Nicholas Nickelbery*. Greatly offended and upset by such cheap imitations that had appeared

---

[16]Samuel Laman Blanchard was the editor of a newspaper, the *True Sun*; Colburn was a publisher, the former partner and now rival of *Oliver Twist*'s publisher, Richard Bentley.

in print and on stage even before the novels were finished running, Dickens tried to protect *Nicholas Nickleby* by publishing a public statement as a separate pamphlet and newspaper advertisement claiming to be the "only true and lawful **Boz**,"[17] and condemning "those dishonest dullards . . . [who]. . . impose on the unwary and credulous by producing cheap and wretched imitations of our delectable Works" (Slater xxix–xxx).[18] Concerns about copyright are also brought up, briefly, but conspicuously and awkwardly, within *Nicholas Nickleby* itself; for instance, in the August, 1838, number, the corrupt MP, Mr. Gregsbury, says that he would never support a bill "giving poor grubbing devils of authors a right to their own property" (*Nicholas Nickleby* 149). The issues of copyright, imitation, and literary originality were clearly very much on Dickens' mind.

Unlike the works of "Bos," Trollope's *Michael Armstrong* cannot really be called an imitation of *Oliver Twist* or *Nicholas Nickleby*, however, because its focus on the industrial North is different from either of those novels; there are also no direct allusions to Dickens in the text (similar names, etc.); and the plot is only generally (good and evil characters in conflict over the fate of a poor boy), not specifically similar. Finally, as even a beginning reader of Victorian fiction knows, Dickens certainly did not have a patent on orphans—the fascination with childhood suffering was a common Victorian theme.

Since Mrs. Trollope's novel was not a direct imitation of one of his works, Dickens' ire towards her seems exaggerated and misplaced. There is no way to know what was in Dickens' mind

---

[17] "Boz" was Dickens' sobriquet in the first few years of his career, derived from the tag line he used for his sketches in the *Morning Chronicle*, therefore had to use for *Sketches by Boz*, and then also used for *Pickwick Papers*, *Oliver Twist*, and *Nicholas Nickleby*; after this, he was so well known under his own name that he no longer used the name "Boz."

[18] See Michael Slater's monograph on "The Composition and Monthly Publication of *Nicholas Nickleby*" (*Nicholas Nickleby* vii–lxxii).

at that time, of course, but the most important question is: what elements of *Michael Armstrong* (besides the physical appearance of the type) would set up comparisons between it and Dickens' works, especially *Oliver Twist* and *Nicholas Nickleby*? As I established in the previous chapter, *Michael Armstrong* was conceived as "something towards attracting the public mind" in favor of "hoped-for factory legislation" (Heineman 170). Using material from her own observations in Manchester and that gleaned from reliable sources, Frances Trollope tried to "awaken the national conscience on behalf of the factory children" with harrowing scenes of dangerous working conditions, much like Dickens would try to awaken sympathies for the hapless child victims of the Yorkshire schools in *Nicholas Nickleby* (Heineman 172). And, as we have seen, Dickens used similar sentimentalist techniques in *Oliver Twist* as an attack on the New Poor Law, and, moreover, he may have planned to write a similar novel in support of factory reform and child labor laws.

Evidence suggests that not only were *Michael Armstrong*'s sentimentalist techniques similar to Dickens', but that its subject matter (factory reform) impinged on literary territory that Dickens had already marked out for himself. Obviously responding to statements in Colburn's letter, shown to him by Blanchard, Dickens made the following statement to Blanchard, in a letter dated February 9, 1839 (the day after the diary entry), about the proposed subject matter of his yet-unwritten next novel, *Barnaby Rudge*:

> That gentleman [Colburn] is quite right in supposing that Barnaby Rudge has nothing to do with factories, or negroes—white, black, or parti-colored. It is a tale of the riots of Eighty, before factories flourished as they did thirty years afterwards, and containing—or intended to contain—no allusion to cotton lords, cotton slaves, or anything that is cotton. (*Letters*, vol. 1, 507)

I deduce that Colburn had defended Mrs. Trollope by arguing that *Michael Armstrong*'s subject matter had not been treated by Dickens, in past or even in projected, novels. Dickens' seeming contempt for the subject matter of factory reform—seen in his extravagantly flippant dismissal of "negroes—black, white, or parti-colored" and "cotton lords, cotton slaves, or anything that is cotton"—had not been not in evidence a few months earlier, when he went to on a tour of the Midlands and North Wales in late October and November, 1838, in order to see the cotton mills.[19]

It is quite possible that Dickens' trip to industrial Manchester was made with the vague idea of writing such a novel in his mind. In fact, the reforming politician and nobleman, Lord Ashley, had, using the poet Edward Fitzgerald as a go-between, offered to have Dickens shown what the cotton mills were like" (Johnson, vol. 1, 225). Moreover, in the October, 1838 issue of *Fraser's* magazine, a notice had appeared that invited Dickens to turn to factory reform as his next subject:

> No one who reads his papers can doubt the excellence of his [Dickens'] disposition. The very choice of his later subjects [the Poor Law, the Yorkshire schools] proves his desire to do good. . . But there is a public crime more vast than either of these, and capable, from its peculiar character, of being put down, in whole or in part by legislative enactment. I mean, the *working little boys and girls to death in the factories.* . . In these matters. . .Mr. Dickens might, without diverging into the thorny path of politics, be of incalculable service to his fellowmen. ("Loose Thoughts" 500)

Immediately after the trip to Manchester, Dickens wrote a letter to Fitzgerald proposing another trip and referring to Lord Ashley's

---

[19]In the discourse surrounding factory reform, workers were often compared to negro slaves (an issue which Catherine Gallagher discusses thoroughly in *The Industrial Reformation of English Fiction*), so the black and white negroes are slaves and factory workers, respectively. I take "parti-colored," however, to be a sarcastic word—referring to black and white in zebra stripes or in spots, not to racially mixed people. The sarcasm of this statement is also evident in Dickens' use of "anything that *is* cotton," rather than "anything that has to do with cotton."

July speech revealing the nightmarish working conditions for child laborers in factories:

> With that nobleman's most benevolent and excellent exertions, and with the evidence which he was the means of bringing forward, I am well acquainted . . . . [W]hat I have seen has disgusted and astonished me beyond all measure. I mean to strike the heaviest blow in my power for these unfortunate creatures, but whether I shall do so in "Nickleby," or wait some other opportunity, I have not yet determined . . . . Will you make known to Lord Ashley (confidentially) my intentions on this subject, and my earnest desire to avail myself . . . of his kind assistance? (*Letters* 483–4)

In spite of these apparently serious intentions, Dickens was to write no novel addressing factory issues until much later in *Hard Times* (1854). According to Dickens' biographer Edgar Johnson, "Dickens could not deal with things still so strange to his imagination as those dust-laden mills and their thunderous machines" (Johnson, vol. 1, 225). While it is possible that Dickens' failure to follow up on such rich potential subject matter may have been due to his artistic limitations, I would like to advance another thesis. Within a few months after Dickens wrote this letter in 1838, Frances Trollope went to Manchester in February of 1839, armed with several letters of introduction to radical reform leaders, and used this visual evidence, together with that gleaned from the *Memoir of Robert Blincoe* (1828), Lord Ashley, the Parliamentary Blue Books, and other sources, to produce *Michael Armstrong* in monthly parts beginning in February, 1839.[20] In December of the same year, Charlotte Elizabeth Tonna began to

---

[20]*The Memoir of Robert Blincoe*, written by John Brown, was the autobiography of mill worker, and gave harrowing accounts of his existence as a parish orphan exploited by the factory system. The *Memoir* has been reprinted in *The Slaughterhouse of Mammon*, a 1992 anthology of Victorian social-protest literature. The Blue Books were reports on the effects of the Industrial Revolution, especially the Sadler Committee's report on children's employment of 1832.

serialize *Helen Fleetwood* in *The Christian Lady's Magazine*. Both of these works became so identified with the factory controversy that any contribution by Dickens would probably have seemed superfluous.

Some contemporary reviewers saw *Michael Armstrong* as an imitation of *Oliver Twist* and *Nicholas Nickleby* because of its focus on exploited children, even though neither one of Dickens' novels has anything to do with the factories that Frances Trollope explores in her novel. One June, 1839, reviewer wrote:

> Boz, like Byron, has his imitators: since the increasing demand for the *Nickleby* article, Boz, not being protected by patent like Mackintosh [the inventor of waterproof cloth], has been pirated; cuckoos lay their eggs in his nest; countless are the Factory-Boys which Mrs. Trollope has turned loose. (Ford 90)

Frances Trollope's biographer, Helen Heineman, tries to argue, on the other hand, that it was Trollope who "boldly led the way in making fiction the 'medium of interpretation' for a new age, and the novel with a purpose rapidly became a common and then a dominant type as the 1840's progressed" (171).[21] The real issue, however, is not who "invented" sentimentalist social reform discourse, if it can even be said to have been invented at all.

My own conclusion is that sentimentalist social reform discourse was too broad, and the product of too many commonly-held cultural values, to be claimed as the intellectual property of any one author. This discourse, as I established in the previous chapter, came from the intersection of two major cultural factors: the breakdown of the moral economy, which resulted from the

---

[21] Heineman makes this argument for Trollope's pre-eminence even at the expense of Charlotte Elizabeth Tonna, who, Heineman believes, "emphasized the wickedness of the workers" at the expense of the "intolerable [working] conditions" (172). Since Tonna's novel, as I demonstrated elsewhere in this book, provided extensive descriptions of poor living and working conditions, especially of children, in support of the Ten Hours Bill, this criticism does not seem accurate or fair.

new material conditions of the industrial era, and the hardening of a domestic ideology that gave women a specifically affective function within those material conditions. The consequence of this cultural "intersection" was that social reform discourse, with its task of using sentiment to creat sympathy for exploited and oppressed groups, was increasingly seen as the province of women writers.

This feminization resulted in a kind of critical depreciation that affected Dickens' own critical reputation—as is evidenced by critical comments like Fitzjames Stephen's previously-quoted statement that Dickens as a politician was (or appealed to) "a feminine, irritable, and noisy mind" (9). Stephen made two other comments in the same article, "Mr. Dickens as a Politician," that obliquely associated Dickens with femininity: "As there are reproaches which can be uttered by no one but a woman or a child, there are accusations which can only be conveyed through a novel," and "But just as a foolish gossip in a country-town, who says what she pleases. . . a popular novelist may produce more disaffection and discontent than a whole army of pamphleteers and public orators . . ." (9). Moreover, Stephen was not the only mid-Victorian critic to make such an observation. Richard Holt Hutton made a milder, but still devastating, remark in the same vein in 1858:

> Indeed, the type of Dickens' genius is, in many respects, feminine. Like most womens' genius, it is founded on the delicate powers of perception alone . . . . There is no intellectual background to his pictures; and in this respect, he resembles the numerous authoresses of modern English fiction. (469)

Hutton was evidently so convinced by the truth of this observation that he repeated it later in the same review, saying that "In all great masculine novel-writers—except Mr. Dickens, who, with all his genius, is in some remarkable points feminine,— you see how good an influence the masculine power of abstraction has on the imagination" (477).

Although the reception of Dickens' works was so clearly entangled in the same gender binaries that affected women writers like Elizabeth Gaskell, he still did his best to fight for his status as an artist by consistently declaring himself an original and women writers the imitators and usurpers. In 1854, for example, Dickens, again in a private letter, attacked another female "imitator." This time, the object of his attack was the American novelist Harriet Beecher Stowe. Publicly, Dickens lauded Stowe's anti-slavery novel *Uncle Tom's Cabin*, calling it in an 1853 speech during Stowe's visit to America "a noble book with a noble purpose" (*Speeches* 165). In 1852, however, he had confided to a friend that he thought Mrs. Stowe had "appropriated" material from his own work and Elizabeth Gaskell's *Mary Barton* (Knight 43):

> She (I mean Mrs. Stowe) is a leetle unscrupulous in the appropriatin' way, I seem to see a writer with whom I am very intimate (and whom nobody can possibly admire more than myself) peeping often through the thinness of the paper. Further I descry the ghost of Mary Barton . . . but in spite of this, I consider the book a fine one...and worthy of its reputation. (Knight 44)

Dickens was probably unaware of Stowe's connections with another author who could more justly than himself lay claim to Stowe. In 1844, several years before writing *Uncle Tom's Cabin*, Stowe edited an American edition of Charlotte Elizabeth Tonna's works. In an introductory essay written for that edition, Stowe explicitly compared Tonna and Dickens, claiming that Tonna's social reform fiction was more practical and effective than Dickens': "This lady's [Tonna's] portrayals of factory life are just illustrations of what such delineations ought to be . . ." (Stowe, Introduction 3). Stowe's acquaintance of Tonna's work clearly put her in full possession of a larger tradition that encompassed Dickens' narrow conception of his own work; Stowe was influenced by Dickens' use of sentiment, but was also influenced by the more overtly religious Tonna, and this indicates the presence of a larger feminized cultural discourse that encompassed both Dickens and Tonna.

Since Stowe herself had told Dickens that he had inspired her work, however, his conclusions are perhaps understandable,[22] but more importantly, the act of declaring himself the original and Stowe the imitator again shows Dickens' attempt to fight the discursive categories being constructed by cultural agents like the *Gentleman's Magazine* review that I discussed in the previous chapter, which designated social morality in literature as a specifically female task, and made sentimentalist social reform discourse a feminized discourse. By arguing that he was the source of this discourse, Dickens tried to deny its gender classification and its depreciation; if he, a male writer, had originated it, then it couldn't be a feminine discourse.

Another method that Dickens may have used to distance himself from female social reformers like Charlotte Elizabeth Tonna is his devastating satire of them, namely in the novel *Bleak House*. Many readers, both contemporary reviewers and later critics, have noted the acidity of Dickens' portrayals of the two "meddling" female philanthropists, Mrs. Jellyby and Mrs. Pardiggle. As Beth Tobin has noted, "Dickens' disdain for these women is so strong that his sarcastic, angry voice displaces Esther's usually diffident, modulated voice" (135). The first of these characters, Mrs. Jellyby, is so involved in her charitable activities (currently centered on a Christian mission to the African country of Borrioboola-Gha) that she ignores her own family and her own home. Her children are neglected to the point of abuse; the house is "not only very untidy, but very dirty" and very poorly run (*Bleak House* 85). Mrs. Pardiggle visits the homes of the poor and makes a nuisance out of herself, distributing religious tracts without doing anything concrete to alleviate the physical misery of those she visits. Meanwhile, her own children are

---

[22]Stowe sent a copy of *Uncle Tom's Cabin* to Dickens, inscribing it to "the first writer in our day who turned the attention of the high to the joys and sorrows of the lowly.... If I may hope to do only something like the same for a class equally ignored and despised by the fastidious and refined in my country, I shall be happy" (*Letters* vol. 6 716).

"absolutely ferocious with discontent" (*Bleak House* 151). These deficiencies are particularly damning in the world of this novel, as "In the emblematic qualities of the characters and of their 'connections' *Bleak House* is an interpretation of Victorian society" (Miller 13). Dickens uses the novel to portray a society that is on the verge of collapse, due to generations of neglect and misuse. This neglect is symbolized by many characters and institutions in the novel, the Court of Chancery, Mr. Turveydrop, and Mr. Skimpole among them, and the fact that Dickens includes Mrs. Jellyby and Mrs. Pardiggle among these represents a serious attack on the activities of charitable women.

The problem with Mrs. Jellyby is that not only do her activities injure her husband, children, and home, but they are ultimately futile and self-serving because they are not based on Mrs. Jellyby's genuine feeling for the causes she supports. Indeed, Dickens implies that the actual cause itself does not matter to Mrs. Jellyby, since "She has devoted herself to an extensive variety of public subjects at various times, and is at present (until something else attracts her) devoted to the subject of Africa . . . " (*Bleak House* 82). When the Africa project becomes a failure due to "the king of Borrioboola wanting to sell everbody . . . for Rum (933), Mrs. Jellyby turns her attention to women's rights, which Dickens implies is yet another futile and worthless project, "involving even more correspondence than the old one" (933).

As Mrs. Pardiggle clearly represents another variation on this theme, *Bleak House* seems to contain nothing but contempt for the "rapacious benovolence" of "the Women of England, the Daughters of Britain, the Sisters of all the Cardinal Virtues separately, the Females of America, the Ladies of a hundred denominations" (150). Dickens contrasts the activities of these businesslike female philanthropists in the novel against the quiet, self-sacrificing, self-effacing, domesticized charity of the heroine, Esther Summerson. Esther's charitable activites are not public and institutionalized but spontaneous, private, and always the result of personal sympathy for those afflicted. For example, Esther's kindness to the Jellyby children, her visits to the brickmakers' cottage, and her taking in the crossing-sweeper, Jo, when he is ill all conform to this model.

In this manner, as Beth Tobin has suggested, Dickens represents a subversion of the more activist model of female charity that is part of what I have labelled as sentimentalist social reform discourse:

> Whereas Hannah More locates in the public sphere a space in which her heroine can exercise her "female benevolent power," Dickens limits his heroine to the domestic sphere. . . . Dickens refuses to bestow his approbation on any woman who extends her realm of influence beyond these boundaries. (Tobin 146–147)

At the same time, Dickens' portrayal of Esther derives in many ways from the feminized, sentimentalist idea that true charity comes from the heart, but in his formulation, this limits Esther's activities to the domestic sphere; in her case, Tonna's "talent of female influence" does not extend very far.

Tobin also argues that "Esther's 'circle of duty' sounds a retreat for women into the domestic sphere and a retirement from public activity and from participating in institutional solutions to social ills" (147). She does not attempt to explain Dickens' motives for sounding this retreat, and it is of course impossible for us to divine the deep-seated psychological reasons that lie behind Dickens' portrayals of his women characters. It is important to point out, however, Dickens was himself involved with many of the same causes as these "meddling" female social reformers, and probably had his own fingers in more charitable pies than Mrs. Jellyby herself.[23] In fact, one of Dickens' sharpest critics, Harriet Martineau, pointed out that "the names of Dickens and Jellyby are joined in a firm as humanity-mongers in the minds of his [Dickens'] readers" ("The Factory Controversy" 45). In addition, Dickens enjoyed a close personal friendship with at least one "meddling" woman philanthropist, Angela Burdett-Coutts, and

---

[23] See Norris Pope's *Dickens and Charity* (1978) for a more detailed account of Dickens' charitable activities, which included the Ragged School movement, sanitary reform, and poor relief.

worked closely with her on some of her charities, namely Urania Cottage, a home she established for the reclamation of prostitutes. Dickens also publicly expressed admiration for many female social reform writers, such as Harriet Beecher Stowe and Elizabeth Gaskell, regardless of what he might have said or thought about them privately. How, then, can we explain these inconsistencies on Dickens' part?

Part of the problem was that, as F. M. Prochaska has suggested, "the view of woman's mission was in flux in the nineteenth century" (1). On one hand, the "separate spheres" philosophy allowed, even encouraged, women towards charitable work: "Free from the cut and thrust of commercial life and thought to be more sensitive to personal relations, women were increasingly called upon to be agents of social improvement" (Prochaska 7). As I have already shown, Charlotte Elizabeth Tonna's idea of "the talent of female influence" was a natural outgrowth of a domestic ideology that assigned women the affective functions of society. On the other hand, there was disagreement about the extent to which women could go in exerting this influence without being thought "unwomanly," as Dickens' satire in *Bleak House* shows. In many ways, the "talent of female influence" could become a trap in which women "willingly reinforced the stereotypes of women as the more compassionate, self-sacrificing sex" because the "claims of women to moral authority and greater social recognition depended on public belief in their special and essential qualities" (Prochaska 8).[24]

My main focus in this chapter, however, is the extent to which Dickens himself was caught up in the cultural expectations set up by the domestic ideology. I have demonstrated that many of Dickens' central themes and literary techniques—his use of illness and other forms of physical suffering to arouse pathos in his audience, his allusions to commonly-held religious beliefs, his understanding of death, even his construction of himself as a preacher who taught his audience their social duties—mark

---

[24] I will argue in the next chapter that Elizabeth Gaskell went on to explore this issue in her novel *North and South*.

Dickens as a part of sentimentalist discourse of social reform. Even Dickens' later novels, which have traditionally been seen as more mature, complex, darker, and less sentimental, display many of these same characteristics.[25] Indeed, *Bleak House* itself, in spite of its satire of women reformers, still makes use of their sentimentalist conventions. Dickens' condemnations of English society in the novel are rhetorical blasts worthy of Charlotte Elizabeth Tonna herself, since they threaten divine retribution for society's tolerance of social ills, and his heart-wrenching descriptions of the poor and downtrodden in the novel have a great deal more in common with Tonna, and other women writers like her, than they do with any of Dickens' male contemporaries, or, for that matter, any of his male precursors.

An understanding of sentimentalist discourse, therefore, is clearly crucial for Dickens critics: it is a "missing piece" that explains much about his fiction that has not yet been properly understood. In his 1987 book *Sacred Tears*, Dickens scholar Fred Kaplan advanced the idea that Dickens' sentimentality derived directly from eighteenth-century moral philosophy, especially as it was exhibited in eighteenth-century novelists like Fielding, Goldsmith, and Richardson, which Dickens certainly read. While his attention to sentimentality as an important, and previously neglected, aspect of Victorian culture is commendable, Kaplan does not deal with the feminization of the eighteenth-century moral sentiments that occured in the nineteenth century. The growing cultural identification of women, with their culturally designated attributes of "religious sensibility and social pity" (Prochaska 7), as ideal charity workers and social reform writers was a key part of the culture in which Dickens was working.

---

[25]My sense is that this critical concentration on Dickens' later fiction is part of a formalist attempt to resuscitate Dickens' reputation by arguing that his later novels "grow out" of the sentimentalist flaws of the earlier novels and become darker and more psychologically complex. See, for example, F. R. and Q. D. Leavis' study of *Dickens the Novelist*, which does not discuss any of Dickens' novels before *Dombey and Son* (1844–6).

How did Victorian society receive a male writer, who, in many respects, wrote like a woman? As I have demonstrated, Dickens' reception was mixed. Although he was darling of the Victorian middle class, and indisputably the most popular of all the Victorian novelists, both male and female, he was still labelled by many of the serious thinkers of his day as "a feminine, irritable, and noisy mind" (Stephen 9). In an age where men were supposed to be men and women were supposed to be women, this was clearly an uncomfortable position to be in, and may in part explain, although of course not excuse, Dickens' sometimes unreasonable attitude towards his female colleagues. Most importantly, however, Dickens' problems as a male sentimentalist indicate first, that sentimentalism was an ideological and aesthetic system to which both Dickens and his female colleagues had access during the Victorian period; second, that the decline of sentimentalism had a negative impact not only on the women writers, but also on Dickens. In the final analysis, however, Dickens' juggernaut-like popularity has enabled his works to overcome these critical vicissitudes with more success than, for example, those of Elizabeth Gaskell.

Chapter Four

"I Know Nothing of Political Economy": Elizabeth Gaskell's Call to Sympathy

Elizabeth Gaskell and Charles Dickens share at least two significant qualities as novelists: namely, an interest in social issues and a corresponding conviction that fiction could change society for the better by influencing the audience. In addition, both authors share a quality that most critics have seen as a weakness: the tendency to deal with social issues in their fiction by resolving conflicts through feminized conventions such as religious conversion and emotional reconciliation.[1] I am arguing that these similarities come not from Gaskell's imitation of Dickens, or vice versa, but from the influence of sentimentalist social reform discourse on both writers—an influence that affected Gaskell's critical reputation even more adversely than it did Dickens'.

Louis Cazamian's condescending statements in his 1903 study *The Social Novel in England: 1830–1870* show how gender binaries influenced the reception of nineteenth-century writers who used sentimentalist conventions as a way to construct social issues. His claim that "it was left to women's gentler and more impulsive imaginations to mark the link between the charitable precepts of Christianity and the duty of social responsibility" repeats and

---

[1]Compare, for example, the way that the death of Stephen Blackpool in Dickens' *Hard Times* (1854) helps to "convert" the Utilitarian Mr. Gradgrind, and how John Barton's deathbed in Gaskell's *Mary Barton* leads to the reconciliation and mutual forgiveness of John Barton and the millowner, Mr. Carson. Of such scenes, Louis Cazamian said, dismissively, that Gaskell contributed to social philosophy by giving a "feminine, Christian interpretation of industrial questions" that was "as little fitted as Dickens to construct an economic alternative to Ricardo" (214). By "feminized," I mean that nineteenth-century readers, like Cazamian, would have been more likely to associate these conventions with women writers.

reinforces the same assumptions about gender roles that I have outlined in the previous two chapters (Cazamian 212). Since women were considered to be "naturally" more "gentle" and "impulsive" ("impulsive" can also be read as "more emotional"), they were the "natural" authors of a discourse that reminded nineteenth-century readers of their charitable responsibilities, but at the same time these women writers were barred from any real artistic recognition.[2]

My analysis of Dickens in chapter three has shown how his work is aligned with this sentimentalist discourse that uses feminized social values to move readers to engage with social problems. In addition, I have argued that Dickens' "cross dressing," his use of conventions that did not match his own physical gender, adversely affected his critical reputation among the intellectuals and literati, both in the nineteenth century and since.

Both Gaskell and Dickens were adversely affected by their identification with sentimentalist social reform discourse, but the effects on Gaskell's reputation have been longer lasting and more severe due to the problems and limitations faced by a woman writer working in the sentimentalist mode. Even though most scholars studying nineteenth-century literature would admit that

---

[2] In his dependence on these assumptions Cazamian follows in the footsteps of critics such as the 1853 *Gentleman's Magazine* reviewer that I quoted in the second chapter:

> Let no one neglect or throw contempt on the impulse which leads the higher classes--high whether in the social or the moral scale--to communicate freely with the lower . . . . our literature and our morals require more and more for their basis a sound increasing knowledge and sympathy between all orders of men. Mutual comprehension--mutual understanding of each other, how inestimable a privilege it is! This is what women can especially forward . . . . (*The Gentleman's Magazine* 24)

In addition, the critical reception of Gaskell's first novel, *Mary Barton*, demonstrates exactly these same assumptions about the suitability of women writers for social reform fiction, as I will demonstrate later in the chapter.

Gaskell's fiction has much merit—she is not attacked on an artistic level as much as writers like Frances Trollope and Tonna are—she still does not receive a proportionate amount of critical attention. For example, the amount of scholarly work devoted to Gaskell is quite minimal compared to the work done on Dickens, even though the two writers have significant similarities, as I have pointed out. More importantly, she has been consistently classified as a "minor" writer, while the reputations of other nineteenth-century novelists shift and move around her (Schor 349). Gaskell's use of sentimentalist discourse was received differently than Dickens' use of the same discursive techniques because there was no slippage between her physical gender and her use of sentimentalist discourse. In fact, her femininity, both in the sense of her physical gender and her public persona, has always been seen as the very essence of her reception as a novelist.[3] It is the femininity embodied in both Gaskell's life and

---

[3] By this I mean that not only was Gaskell a woman in the physical sense, she was also a "womanly woman" who did not use a male pseudonym, wear male clothing, or flout social conventions with an unconventional lifestyle, as did other nineteenth-century women writers like George Eliot and George Sand. Instead, she was described by contemporaries as "pretty" and "sweet," and (apparently) fulfilled the conventional expectations of a clergyman's wife and the mother of several daughters. In addition, her "public persona" was really characterized by her lack of one--she seemed to make every effort to keep her private life to herself, was very concerned about the anonymity of *Mary Barton*, refused to allow anyone to write her biography, etc. But this attitude, conspicuously conventional in an age were women's names were supposed to appear in the newspaper only at their birth, marriage, and death, was in itself a public persona. Moreover, the effects of this persona were tenacious; for instance, by the fact that until quite recently, Gaskell was often still known as "Mrs. Gaskell," while other major nineteenth-century female novelists were known either by their full names or their male pseudonyms (e.g.; "Charlotte Brontë," "Jane Austen," "George Eliot," etc.).

work, Gaskell scholars argue, that has resulted in her reputation as a "second rate" novelist: as critic Hilary Schor has pointed out, "Gaskell's 'charm,' to use a word . . . occasionally used to dismiss her, is so intensely gender-coded as to make it impossible for her ever to acquire 'major' status" (349).[4] Other Gaskell scholars, namely Edgar Wright, have maintained that it was Gaskell's attention to social reform issues in her works that prevented her from achieving literary excellence. Gaskell seems to have moved away from social reform issues later in her career, and Wright has argued that she failed to achieve excellence as an artist until she abandoned these issues.[5] I am contending, however, that this shift in subject matter is due to her realization that she would never be recognized as an artist until she broke away from the confining gender binaries that constrained her audience's understanding of social reform fiction by women writers.[6] Like Elizabeth Barrett

---

[4]Schor does not address Dickens' own problems with gender stereotyping.

[5]Edgar Wright argues in *Elizabeth Gaskell: The Basis for Reassessment* (1965) that Gaskell's subject matter, factory reform, was largely responsible for her failure to achieve artistic recognition, and that it was only after she abandoned the industrial world of Manchester in her fiction that she produced "the best of her work": "Her remaining fiction...carried steadily fewer traces of being written with a sense of obligation towards ideals of moral or public duty, and this freedom . . . is reflected in the range and tone of what she produced" (146).

[6]This dilemma can also be seen in the experience of Charlotte Brontë, who published *Shirley*, her only novel dealing with industrial issues, in 1849. In order to avoid the stigma of topicality that caused novels like *Mary Barton*, Frances Trollope's *Michael Armstrong*, Tonna's *Helen Fleetwood*, and Elizabeth Stone's *William Langshawe, Cotton Lord* not to be taken seriously as art, Brontë set *Shirley* in the Luddite period (1811–12) instead of the eighteen-forties and made overt claims for the novel's realism: "Do you anticipate sentiment, and poetry, and reverie? . . . Something real, cool, and solid, lies before you; something unromantic as Monday morning . . ." (*Shirley* 5). By claiming that

Browning, Gaskell used the conventions of sentimentalist discourse in order to align herself with the feminized social values that made Charlotte Elizabeth Tonna's "female influence" so effective—writing from this moralistic, impassioned, Christian perspective gave her a stance that enabled her to speak effectively as a woman, but this same stance barred her from artistic recognition. In the final analysis, it is neither Gaskell's "charm," nor only her subject matter that doomed her critical stature, but a fatal combination of the two that made her audience read her fiction according to the feminized conventions of sentimentalist social reform discourse.

Gaskell's first novel, *Mary Barton*, was published in 1848 towards the end of the "hungry forties," when concern over the gulf between the rich and the poor, the employers and the employed, was at its height. Married to a Unitarian clergyman and a resident of Manchester, Gaskell had a fairly intimate acquaintance with factory issues, and was a natural candidate for writing a novel that, like Tonna's *Helen Fleetwood* and Frances Trollope's *Michael Armstrong*, would arouse audience sympathies for the factory workers and help to reconcile the "two nations" of the rich and the poor. As I have already established, her

---

her novel represented something more real than "harrowing up my reader's soul . . . with effective descriptions of stripes and scourgings" (*Shirley* 62), Brontë explicitly positions herself against sentimentalist social reform writers whose novels depended on detailed, dramatic depictions of physical suffering in order to win their readers' sympathies and awaken their consciences. Even with these precautions, however, *Shirley* was still reviewed by George Henry Lewes on the basis of its author's gender, which greatly upset and angered Brontë. Christine Krueger, in her discussion of this episode, notes the significance of the fact that "Brontë's first, and only, social problem novel" inspired "Lewes to treat the subject of the author's sex" (231). It is interesting to note that in spite of Gaskell's intent to concentrate more on Charlotte Brontë, the woman, than on Currer Bell, the novelist, her biography of Brontë does relate this episode in detail, and quotes in full Brontë's two letters to Lewes responding to this review.

femininity, if nineteenth-century literary criticism is anything to go by, would have been more of a help than a hindrance to her in this task.

Elizabeth Gaskell, however, was quite determined that *Mary Barton* should not be published under her own name. She searched for a male pseudonym up to the time of its publication, considering and rejecting her previous pseudonym, "Cotton Mather Mills," and a new name, "Stephen Berwick," as possible candidates. Finally, *Mary Barton* was published anonymously on October 18, 1848.[7] This anonymity was not the result of advice from Chapman and Hall, who seem to have been indifferent on this point, or from Gaskell's friend and negotiator, William Howitt, who advised her to publish the novel under her own name. Well known in radical literary and political circles, Howitt had published a few of Gaskell's earlier short stories in his new reformist magazine, *Howitt's Journal*.[8] He wrote Gaskell that "it seems to me that as you will write (I trust many) other works, it would be as well for them to be known as the works of a lady. I think that they would be more popular . . ." (Uglow 183). Howitt, who had urged Gaskell to "use her pen for the public benefit" (Krueger 170), was probably quite familiar with the power of a feminine voice in the arena of social reform debate, and his belief that Gaskell's novel would be more popular if it were known to be by a woman is suggestive of the cultural assumptions that the Victorian audience had about social reform literature by women

---

[7] As Edgar Wright notes in his introduction to the Oxford World's Classics edition of *Mary Barton*, "the date normally given is 25 October [1848], but [J. G.] Sharps argues persuasively for 18 October" (xxv); I agree with the earlier date, because it explains how the *Athenaeum* would have already been able to provide a review of the novel on October 21, 1848.

[8] According to Gaskell's most recent biographer, Jenny Uglow, "*Howitt's Journal* contained every kind of radicalism, its varied ingredients boiled down into a rather bland soup with a dominant flavour of romantic, high-minded reformism, salted by Samuel Smiles' self-help. It set out to entertain, but nothing could disguise its didactic taste" (171).

authors. Gaskell did not follow his advice, however, and it is clear that she did not want *Mary Barton* to be identified as "the work of a lady," since she refused to acknowledge "authorship until after it had been guessed by most of her friends and several critics" (Krueger 170).[9]

In spite of Gaskell's desire for anonymity and androgyny, however, *Mary Barton* contained many features in common with sentimentalist social reform writers like Tonna, showing Gaskell's indebtedness to the powerful, but feminized, sentimentalist discourse of social reform established by other women writers. This allegiance was evident even in the preface to *Mary Barton*, where Gaskell claimed political and narrative authority as an impartial, but sympathetic, observer: "I know nothing of Political Economy, or the theories of trade. I have tried to write truthfully; and if my accounts agree or clash with any system, the agreement or disagreement is unintentional" (*Mary Barton* xxxvi). This deceptively ingenuous and self-deprecating statement is actually quite effective. Gaskell suggests with the carefully capitalized "Political Economy" and the word "theories" that these viewpoints are abstract and removed from the reality that her account "truthfully" and "unintentionally" records without serving a motive of its own. As Christine Krueger has established, Gaskell's statement "[strikes] at the root of abstract discourses which claim to base their authority on claims of empirical evidence while remaining remote from experience" (172).[10]

Gaskell did actually know quite a bit about political economy, but instead of fighting theories with counter-theories, she used the emotionalism of sentimentalist discourse to move her readers by showing the miseries that industrial capitalism had caused.

---

[9]JennyUglow, concurs with the conclusion that Gaskell wanted to avoid the stereotyping that came with the feminine label: "[S]he was reluctant to be identified with the book and did not want it to seem 'the work of a lady" (171).

[10]Krueger also concurs with Patsy Stoneman in identifying these "abstract discourses as masculine" (Krueger 172, Stoneman 41).

Gaskell stated this intention to awaken "the sympathy of the happy" in the novel's preface:

> The more I reflected on this unhappy state of things between those so bound to each other by common interests, as the employers and employed must ever be, the more anxious I became to give some utterance to the agony which, from time to time, convulses these dumb people [the factory workers], the agony of suffering without the sympathy of the happy, or of erroneously believing that such is the case. If it be an error that the woes which . . . overwhelm the workmen in our manufacturing towns pass unregarded by all but the sufferers, it is at any rate an error so bitter in its consequences to all parties, that whatever public effort can do in the way of legislation, or private effort in the way of merciful deeds . . . should be done . . . . (*Mary Barton* xxxvi)

Although Gaskell initially kept her identity and gender secret and published the novel anonymously, she implicitly aligned herself in this preface with the feminized social values, like sympathy, that made Tonna's "female influence" so effective. For instance, she also said in the Preface that the novel was an emotional manifestation of her "deep sympathy" for the workers (*Mary Barton* xxxv). On the other hand, Gaskell's stance was less strident and accusing than Tonna's: for example, she hedged about her middle-class audience's responsibility for the bitterness of the workers when she implied that the workers' belief that they suffer without "the sympathy of the happy" may have been in error.[11] She never actually said that it was an error, though, and

---

[11] Compare this passage to one from Tonna's *The Wrongs of Woman* (1843–44) where Tonna addresses her middle-class female audience's complicity with the exploitation of young seamstresses:

> How . . . dwelleth the love of Christ in us if we connive at the cruel oppression exercised over the helpless young females of our land? How dare we profess His holy Name, and assume to be partakers in the joy of his salvation, while lending ourselves to this worst of wrong and robbery, the wrong and robbery of the poor? Is this the mind that was in Christ Jesus? There is one female named, who went forth to the dance, as one of courtly splendour, and elicited even royal applause, while captivating a throng of nobles by her external appearance; yet, who, in that very moment, brought upon her soul the guilt of innocent blood. May

her intent to inspire her audience to "merciful deeds or helpless love in the way of widow's mites" (*Mary Barton* xxxvi) was very similar to Tonna's desire to influence her audience's behavior.

In spite of the religious differences between Gaskell and Tonna, Gaskell's preface also uses the same kinds of "feminized" religious values that Tonna used in her works, and Gaskell attributes her concerns in *Mary Barton* to these values when she states her belief that the workers' bitterness "taints what might be resignation to God's will" (*Mary Barton* xxxv).[12] This concern for her subjects' moral and religious welfare is a common thread that runs from Hannah More and Tonna. In fact, More expresses more concern for the spiritual well being of the poor than she does for their physical health; in many places she even implies that physical suffering is necessary for their spiritual welfare. Tonna, on the other hand, is sincerely concerned about the physical suffering of the poor, but one of the most important reasons for this concern is her fear that physical suffering will alienate the poor from the religious faith that she believes is necessary for their salvation. For example, in this passage from "The Little Pin Headers" Tonna expresses her fear that child laborers will become alienated from Christ, "The Children's Friend":

> Ah, lady, take from any part of your apparel that very trivial though indispensable appendage, a common pin: look well upon it, and then I will show you another picture: I will show you the professed disciples of the Lord Jesus not merely barring the way by which mothers might bring their little ones to Him for the blessing that he waits to bestow, but opening a way . . . by which they [the mothers] must carry those little ones to the brink of a pit, and fling them, helpless, hopeless, succourless, into the iron grasp of Satan. (*Wrongs* 7)[13]

> God, in His rich mercy, deliver the daughters of England from such a snare!" (*Wrongs* 107–8).

[12]Gaskell was a liberal Unitarian; Tonna was a strongly conservative Evangelical Anglican.

[13]Later on in "The Little Pin Headers," one of the four sections of *The Wrongs of Woman*, Tonna deals at length with the religious ignorance of the child laborers.

In addition, of course, Tonna's concern for the poor's spiritual welfare appeals to the conventional religious values of her audience, a strategy which Gaskell also uses in her preface to *Mary Barton* with her worry about the workers' "resignation to Gods' will" (*Mary Barton* xxxv).

Admirers of *Mary Barton* have tended to express their admiration by distancing it from the industrial novels of other women writers like Tonna and claiming its artistic superiority over Tonna's more overtly religious and didactic works,[14] but as we have seen, even the novel's brief preface shows a rhetorical stance that is commensurate with sentimentalist discourse, and this use of sentimentalist assumptions and conventions is also borne out in the novel itself.

Like Tonna, Gaskell uses a didactic, explicitly preacher-like, even Biblical, narrative voice to interject commentary into the novel's action:

> But remember! we only miss those who do men's work in their humble sphere; the aged, the feeble, the children when they die, are hardly noted by the world; and yet to many hearts, their deaths make a blank which long years will never fill up . . . . The people had thought the poverty of the preceding years hard to bear, and had found its yoke hard, but this year added sorely to its weight. Former times had chastised them with whips, but this chastised them with scorpions. (*Mary Barton* 130)

Cazamian differentiates between Tonna and Gaskell by saying that "unlike Tonna . . . [Gaskell] could argue without sectarian

---

[14]Louis Cazamian, for instance, contrasts *Mary Barton*'s "truthful realism" and "convincing, individual" characters with the "mediocre literary quality" of *Helen Fleetwood* (231, 240). This literary judgment reappears in the work of more recent critics, such as Joseph Kestner, who says that Gaskell, "unlike . . . Tonna, and Trollope, refrains from indictments, avoiding the artificiality caused by overwriting" (*Protest and Reform* 117). Indeed, the whole thesis of Monica Fryckedstedt's 1980 article on *Mary Barton* and the early industrial novel is to show that "Mrs. Gaskell's greater artistry . . . places her in a category beyond her many predecesors," including Tonna (12).

and theological dogmatism" (116). There is a great deal of truth to this statement, but as Christine Krueger has more astutely noted, both Tonna and Gaskell use the same didactic preacher voice in which the narrator addresses the audience directly in order to teach them something important. Gaskell uses the imperative in the first sentence of this passage, and then she infuses Biblical language and imagery into subsequent sentences in order to claim religious and moral authority; the last sentence alludes to King Rehoboam's reply to the beleaguered children of Israel who dare to ask for better treatment: "My father chastised you with whips, but I will chastise you with scorpions" (I Kings 12:11).

As I argued earlier in this book, this use of biblical authority is a key part of sentimentalist discourse, which influences the reader not only through pathos but through the whole "feminine" system of moral and religious values that the pathos epitomizes, a value system exemplified by both the urgent preaching of a narrator and emotional enactments of Christian eschatology. In the nineteenth century, the "separate spheres" philosophy meant that the application of these Christian values to economic and political issues was a feminized technique, which Louis Cazamian's statement that "it was left to women's gentler and more impulsive imaginations to mark the link between the charitable precepts of Christianity and the duty of social responsibility" makes clear (212).

Even the most casual reading of *Mary Barton* and *Helen Fleetwood*, however, will reveal that *Mary Barton* is much less "preachy" than the earlier novel, although as I have said, it does make use of narrative didacticism to a greater extent than has been previously recognized. The reason why there is less overt narrative commentary in *Mary Barton* is that instead of simply presenting the need for sympathy and charity to the audience as Tonna does, Gaskell tries to enact sympathy and charity within the plot of the novel itself. The ending of Tonna's *Helen Fleetwood* is tragic; almost all of the Greens are dead because of their poor living and working conditions in M (Manchester), and the novel's last words, although spoken by one of the characters, are obviously directed to the audience:

> [W]e should pray for those men who are trying to make the factory children less miserable, and whenever you speak to the great folks, put in a word: for I can't help thinking God must be angry with them while they take so much care about their own little ones, and have no thought, no feeling, for the perishing children of the poor! (428)

Tonna's strategy, in *Helen Fleetwood* and in her other works, is to present pictures of suffering and to give her audience quite explicit instructions on what to do about it. She wants her largely female audience to "use their influence over their own husbands, fathers, brothers, and friends to . . . support our cause [factory reform] in Parliament" (*Helen Fleetwood* 326), so charity and sympathy are not presented in the novels themselves but are presumably left up to the audience.[15]

Gaskell's approach (while not necessarily more effective for social reform purposes) is more subtle, but it still makes use of the conventions of sentimentalist discourse even though the rhetorical strategy is slightly different. *Mary Barton* does present detailed portrayals of physical and emotional suffering, but it also models ways to alleviate that suffering in the text. One example of this modelling is the episode in Chapter VI, appropriately titled "Poverty and Death," where John Barton and his friend George Wilson try to do something about the desperate situation of a fellow factory hand, Davenport, who has been put out of work by the fire at Carson's mill. The two men make their way to the filthy slum where Davenport and his family are now living, and which is described in graphic detail by Gaskell:

---

[15]In fact, Tonna's seeming to desert her characters by leaving them to suffer and die in the mills has been misunderstood by at least one critic. Helen Heineman, in her critical biography of Tonna's contemporary, Frances Trollope, has argued that *Helen Fleetwood* portrays factory working conditions as "inevitable and permanent," only to be remedied by "an inward turning to Christ" (172). Heineman clearly misunderstands Tonna's intent and her strategy: Tonna's motive was in fact the same as the one Heineman attributes to Trollope, "to awaken the national conscience on the behalf of the factory children" (172).

> As they [Barton and Wilson] passed, women from their doors tossed household slops of every description into the gutter; they ran into the next pool, which overflowed and stagnated. . . . Our friends were not dainty, but even they picked their way, till they got to some steps leading down . . . . into the cellar in which a family of human beings lived. It was very dark inside. The window panes were many of them broken and stuffed with rags, which was reason enough for the dusky light that pervaded the place even at mid-day. . . . Quickly recovering themselves, as those inured to such things do, they began to penetrate the thick darkness of the place, and to see three or four little children rolling on the damp, nay wet, brick floor, through which the stagnant, filthy moisture of the street oozed up; the fireplace was empty and black . . . (66–67)

The point of this passage, of course, is to make Gaskell's middle-class readers see the sights and smell the smells that make up the Davenports' desperate living conditions. In this documention of conditions in order to inform and influence the audience, Gaskell follows the tradition of Tonna.

Instead of stopping there to tell her readers that they need to do something about these conditions as Tonna would, however, Gaskell then shows what Barton and Wilson, who by the standards of most of Gaskell's readers are only slightly less poor than the Davenports, do to deal with the situation. Barton runs home and pawns his coat and silk handkerchief in order to buy food, candles, and fuel. Meanwhile, Wilson nurses the family, who are all sick either from starvation or from typhus, and then goes to the home of the mill owner, Mr. Carson, in order to get an infirmary order by which to get Davenport admitted to the hospital.[16] The Carson home, in eloquent contrast to the Davenports', is "furnished with disregard to expense" (74–75), and Wilson also sees a plentiful supply of food available not only to the Carson family but also to their large staff of servants. The Carsons, father and son, respond favorably, but carelessly, to

---

[16]Even though Gaskell portrays Barton and Wilson as performing actions culturally designated as feminine—nursing, cooking, child care—she herself does not call these actions feminine. Her readers, however, did. Kingsley's review of *Mary Barton*, for example, said that the poor in the novel were "kind and sympathising as women to each other" (430).

Wilson's request. Mr. Carson gives Wilson not the necessary in-patient's order, but an out-patient's order, and his son, Harry Carson, gives Wilson five shillings on the way out the door, a much smaller amount than what his father intends to spend on an expensive rosebush for daughter Amy. Wilson's visit, from the Carson point of view, is a minor interruption into the frivolity and comfort of their day, whereas its real urgency is shown again at the end of the chapter when Davenport dies before he can use Carson's out-patient's order, leaving his wife and children to be supported by the parish.

In this chapter, Gaskell models charity in the actions of Barton and Wilson, both of whom, as I have said, would have been considered by most of her readers to be only slightly less poor than the Davenports. Barton and Wilson give generously from the little they have—Wilson is unemployed and his family is living off the wages of his son Jem and Barton can only get short hours because of hard economic times limiting the output of the mill where he works. In contrast, the wealthy Mr. Carson and his largely idle son and daughters do very little, if anything, to help the Davenports. Like Tonna, Gaskell draws on the religious values of sentimentalist discourse in her allusion to the Biblical parable of Dives and Lazarus to portray the gulf in between the rich and the poor.[17]

---

[17]The story of Dives and Lazarus illustrates one aspect of Jesus' teachings on wealth and poverty:

> There was a rich man, who was clothed in purple and fine linen and who feasted sumptuously every day. And at his gate lay a poor man named Lazarus, full of sores, who desired to be fed with what fell from the rich man's table; moreover, the dog came and licked his sores. The poor man died and was carried by the angels to Abraham's bosom. The rich man also died and was buried; and in Hades, being in torment, he lifted up his eyes, and saw Abraham far off and Lazarus in his bosom. And he called out, "Father Abraham have mercy on me, and send Lazarus to dip the end of his finger in water and cool my tongue; for I am in anguish in this flame." But Abraham said, "Son, remember that you in your lifetime received your good things, and Lazarus in like manner evil things; but now he is comforted here, and you are in anguish. "(Luke 16:19-25)

Monica Fryckedstedt has established the similarities between this chapter of Mary Barton and the episode in *Helen Fleetwood* where Mrs. Green goes to the home of Mr. Z, the mill owner, for his help in alleviating Helen's situation at the mill. Unlike Carson, Mr. Z responds not only with ignorance but with hostility. The daughter of Mr. Z, who is totally ignorant about working conditions at the mill, feels "kind commiseration" for Mrs. Green's description of Helen's sufferings, but doesn't do anything about them (173). Tonna obviously disapproves of this neglect, later telling her audience that middle-class women like Amelia Z could be usefully employed teaching the factory children "religious and useful knowledge" (*Helen Fleetwood* 223–24). Gaskell, on the other hand, does not directly address the audience but gets the same point across with the contrast between the actions of Barton and Wilson and the relative inaction of the Carsons. She does not condemn the Carsons, nor portray them as villains incapable of charity; instead, they are a fairly typical wealthy middle-class family, generous in small and careless ways, but not in sustained attention to the suffering poor around them, with whom they have very little sympathy, mostly because of ignorance.

Tonna attempts to create sympathy (and with it charity) with her constant admonitions to her audience, but Gaskell tries a different strategy: her plot forces the Carsons out of the ignorance and complacency that cause their lack of true sympathy for those around them. After young Harry Carson draws a cruel caricature of the desperate trade union leaders (among them John Barton), an action which demonstrates his failure to see their suffering in human terms, the group draw lots in order to see who will kill him. John Barton is the appointed murderer. After Jem Wilson is charged, tried, and acquitted of Barton's crime, Barton, now mortally ill and consumed by guilt, confesses to Mr. Carson in order to try and clear Jem (of whose trial and acquittal he is ignorant).

This twist in the plot sets up a psychodrama in which Carson and Barton, with the help of religious conversion, come to understand, sympathize with, and forgive each other. Witnessing the genuine grief of Mr. Carson forces Barton to come to terms with the human effects of his crime: "The eyes of John Barton grew dim with tears. . . . The sympathy for suffering, formerly so prevalent a feeling with him, again filled [his] heart" (431). Barton's remorse-filled explanation of his action has a similar effect on Carson: "In spite of his desire to retain the revengeful feeling he considered as a duty to his dead son, something of pity would steal in for the poor, wasted skeleton of a man, the smitten creature, who had told him of his sin, and implored his pardon that night" (436). The two men, by witnessing each other's suffering, are moved to sympathy through their emotional responses.

In addition, they are also influenced by the Christian biblical values typical of sentimentalist discourse, since their "conversion experiences" come about through their re-discovery of the revealed truth of the Bible. Both men have been alienated from these values: Barton confesses that he has "dropped down, down—down" (438) since giving up his belief in the Bible, and the Carson family Bible has "leaves adhering together from the bookbinder's press, so little has it been used" (435). After Carson's initial rejection of Barton's plea for forgiveness, the two men go through parallel conversion experiences: while Carson rediscovers his Bible by rereading it, Barton orally repents of his fall away from the Bible in his deathbed monologue to Job Legh, Mary, and Jem. In Gaskell's model, then, the creation of sympathetic emotions is inextricably linked to "natural" human sympathy and to religious conversion, both of which combine to form the change of heart that is so central to the sentimentalist world view. As Jane Tompkins has argued in her analysis of Stowe's *Uncle Tom's Cabin*, the sentimentalist value system reverses "the ordinary or 'commonsense' view of what is efficacious (a view to which most modern critics are committed)" (128) so that according to Stowe's system of values:

> it is the *modern* view that is naive. The political and economic measures that constitute effective action for us, she regards as superficial, mere extensions of the worldly policies that produced the slave system in the first place. . . . She recommends not specific alterations in the current political and economic arrangements, but rather a change of heart. (132)

Much the same could presumably be said about *Mary Barton*, since some contemporary readers, namely Dickens, perceived the influence of *Mary Barton* in Stowe's novel (*Letters of Charles Dickens*, vol. VI, 808).

More importantly, Gaskell's presentation of Carson's change of heart connects it to the experience of reading. Initially rejecting Barton's plea for forgiveness and Jem's quotation from the Lord's prayer, "Forgive us our trespasses as we forgive them that trespass against us" (432), Carson blasphemes by replying, "Let my trespasses be unforgiven, so that I may have vengeance for my son's murder" (433). On his way home, however, he is confronted by another incident that reminds him of the biblical precepts he learned as a child: he sees a little girl refuse to allow a policeman to arrest an errand boy who injured her by accident because, as she says, "He did not know what he was doing" (434). Carson decides to read the New Testament when he gets home, and the experience transforms him:

> Then he ... turned to the object of his search—the Gospel, where he half expected to find the tender pleading: "They know not what they do." .... Years ago, the Gospel had been his task-book in learning to read, so many years ago, that he had become familiar with the events before he could comprehend the Spirit that made the Life. He fell to the narrative now, afresh, with all the interest of a little child. He began at the beginning, and read on almost greedily, understanding for the first time the full meaning of the story. He came to the end: the awful End. And there were the haunting words of pleading.
>
> He shut the book, and thought deeply.
>
> All night long, the Archangel combated with the Demon. (436)

This passage indicates that the experience of reading the Gospel causes Carson's conversion experience, the creation of sympathetic emotions in him, and then a change in his behavior. The next day, Carson is able to forgive Barton, and his conduct towards his workers improves thereafter:

> Many of the improvements now in practice in the system of employment in Manchester, owe their origin to short, earnest sentences spoken by Mr. Carson. Many and many yet to be carried into execution take their birth from that stern, thoughtful mind, which submitted to be taught by suffering. (458)

The word "suffering" in this passage cannot only refer to Carson's own suffering over the death of his son because if that were the case, then his character would have changed for the better directly after his son's death. It also must refer, therefore, to his exposure to Barton's suffering, and his vicarious experience of Christ's suffering in that fateful reading of the Bible.

Why does this presentation of Carson's transformation particularly highlight the importance of reading? His counterpart John Barton is shown remembering the Bible, but not actually reading the Bible.

The key lies in Carson's middle-class status, and his function in the novel as a representative of middle-class indifference to working-class suffering. Since the purpose of *Mary Barton* as a whole is to represent "the agony of suffering without the sympathy of the happy" and to accomplish some kind of change by giving utterance to this suffering, Carson's literary conversion experience is probably the most important moment in the entire novel (*Mary Barton* xxxvi). Gaskell's strategy is to convert her readers by modelling sympathy and charity in the novel's text (as well as by prompting with narrative intervention and biblical allusion), so this moment, where Carson acquires the emotions of sympathy through reading, is clearly the capstone of this strategy. Gaskell invites her readers to put themselves in the place of Carson, to be "converted" by the text of the novel, even as Carson is converted by reading the Bible. In effect, *Mary Barton* becomes a substitute for the Bible itself. Gaskell's novel therefore claims the religious authority that is one of the main strengths of sentimentalist discourse; it is the same authority that Tonna claims with her interjected sermons and biblical allusions. This authority, based on the notion that "historical change takes place only through religious conversion" (Tompkins 511), was particularly credible coming from women writers, since the separate spheres philosophy gave women special access to moral and spiritual values.

Gaskell was clearly influenced by this feminized, sentimentalist cultural discourse of social reform, but her search for a male pseudonym and her desire to remain anonymous and androgynous indicates that she did not wish to be identified with it. Gaskell herself had two main hopes about how her novel would be received: she was "(above every other considerations) desirous that it should be *read*" (*Letters* 56) and, as I pointed out earlier, she did not want it to be read as the work of a woman. In the first goal, she succeeded; in the second, she failed dismally. Gaskell did not keep her book completely secret while it was being written, of course, and the failure of her friends and relatives to keep their mouths shut probably had as much to do with the eventual revelation of her identity as anything. What is significant, however, is the way that most of the novels' reviewers claimed that they were able to identify Gaskell's gender from the text of the novel itself. Her femininity, in other words, became naturalized in the novel's reception.

Mary Barton was reviewed in most, if not all, of the major journals, magazines, and newspapers of the time. The literary and cultural world immediately seized upon it as a significant political contribution to the "Condition of England" debate, even as Stowe's *Uncle Tom's Cabin* was to crystallize the debate over slavery in America. Gaskell herself recognized what this topicality offered for her novel's potential reception, although she did not see *Mary Barton* as propaganda *per se*. In fact, she wrote at least two letters to Chapman and Hall urging them to expedite the novel's publication in order to take advantage of its topicality.[18]

---

[18]On March 21, 1848, Gaskell wrote to Chapman that:

> I am naturally a little anxious to know when you are going to press. I cannot help fancying that the tenor of my tale is such as to excite attention at the present time of struggle on the part of the work people to obtain what they esteem their rights. (*Letters* 54)

Less than two weeks later, not having received an answer from Chapman, she wrote again:

> ... I hope you will not think me impatient in expressing my natural wish to learn when you are going to press, as I think the present state of public events may not be unfavourable to a tale, founded in some measure on the presen[t] relations between Masters and work people. (*Letters* 55)

Both letters refer to the upheavals on the Continent, and Gaskell's

In this regard, *Mary Barton* was a success—it was popular, and some critical perspectives lauded it as an important contribution to the political and social debate about class relations.

Charles Kingsley's review for *Fraser's Magazine*, for example, hailed it as the most important contribution thus far:

> Do they want to know why? Then let them read *Mary Barton*. Do they want to know why poor men, kind and sympathizing as women to each other, learn to hate law and order, Queen, Lords and Commons, country-party, and corn-law leaguer all alike—to hate the rich, in short? Then let them read *Mary Barton* . . . . Lastly, if they want to know why men learn to hate the Church and the Gospell [sic], why then turn sceptics, Atheists, blasphemers, and cry out in the blackness of despair and doubt, 'Let us curse God and die,' let them read *Mary Barton*. (430)[19]

Even in this short passage, however, it is clear that Kingsley praises the novel for political rather than literary reasons. Early in the review, he sets the issue of literary merit aside entirely: "We might praise the 'talent' of this book . . . but the matter puts the manner out of sight" (439). Like *Uncle Tom's Cabin* would in the next decade, *Mary Barton* became not a novel, but the expression of an issue. Unlike Stowe, who evaded the whole question of artistry with her assertions that she wrote *Uncle Tom's Cabin* under divine influence, Gaskell claimed to have put a great deal of thought into the novel's construction, and was upset by the ways in which it was misperceived: "How little she intended the book for political propaganda appears from her early view of it as a 'tragic poem' in the Wordsworthian acceptance of the term, but no one . . . judged the book as that" (Gérin 88). This gendered

---

belief that public interest in whether a similar revolution could occur in England would directly influence the fortunes of her novel.

[19] *Fraser's* had published a lengthy article only two months before on education as a way to elevate the moral conditions of the manufacturing poor, which is probably one of the reasons why it seized on *Mary Barton*, as a confirmation of the views presented in the article.

misreading would not have been a problem for Charlotte Elizabeth Tonna, who had no interest in the literary establishment since she regarded fiction as sinful unless it was used for religious instruction. Gaskell's tragedy, however, was that she wanted to be read as an artist; instead, because of the feminizing influence of sentimentalist discourse, she was read as an "evangelist of reconciliation" (Krueger 157).

The contemporary critics, both public and private, read *Mary Barton* not only as political propaganda (for the most part), they also read it in explicitly feminine terms. Many of the reviewers mention the gender of the author, and they also claim that this knowledge comes naturally from the text of the novel, and not from any outside information about the author's identity. Within a month of the novel's publication, for example, Gaskell received a personal letter about the novel from Thomas Carlyle (whom she had not previously met) addressing her as "Dear Madam, (For I catch the treble of that fine melodious voice very well). . . A beautifully, cheerfully pious, social, clear and observant character is everywhere recognisable in the writer . . ." (Gérin 89). Gaskell suspected that Carlyle had discovered her gender from her gossiping London relatives (Uglow 217), but his letter claimed that he recognized her gender from the "cheerfully pious" "character" of the novel itself.

This naturalization of nineteenth-century assumptions about literature and gender are also evident in the novel's official reviews, especially in the more negative ones. The very earliest review, in *The Athenaeum* on October 21, 1848, only put the writer's gender (literally) in question—"Only twice has he (?) had recourse to the worn-out machinery of the novelist. . ."—and was basically positive in its praise of "the display of character, in the lifelike and simple use of dialogue" (1050).[20] The *British Quarterly Review*, in February 1849, stated that "In the love portion of the story, there is a great deal that indicates the delicate touch of a female hand" (131), but did not elaborate on this observation.

---

[20]This kind of qualification was unusual, as most nineteenth-century literary reviews used "he," even if the author was unknown.

The reviewer also, however, had negative things to say about the novel's close as "twisted out of shape, to serve the didactic purposes of the author" (128); about John Barton's confession scene, which is "forced and unnatural, and tricked out with a quantity of sentimental flourishes" (128); and about the author's "hankering after death scenes" (131). Since all of these flaws are associated with sentimentalist social reform discourse, it doesn't seem too much of a leap to surmise that they are also linked to the author's gender, even though the reviewer does not make these connections explicitly. This review also demonstrates the contempt that many in the literary establishment had for women writers with "didactic purposes," and illustrates perfectly the double-edged sword that threatened these women writers. Even while critics had respect for these writers' goals and motives, the very emotionalism and didacticism that ensured their effectiveness as public consciences often doomed them to critical obscurity.

The reviews of *Mary Barton* also assume the readers do not need to have the feminine "identity" of *Mary Barton* explained, or supported. W. R. Greg's lengthy discussion in the venerable *Edinburgh Review* says only that "*Mary Barton* is understood to be, **and indeed very palpably is**, the production of a lady" without further addressing the issue (208, emphasis added). Evidently, both Greg and his audience know what makes a novel "the production of a lady" without Greg's having to explain it. The same critical move occurs in The *North British Review*, which states that "there is **internal** evidence of a lady's pen," without saying what that evidence is or why and how it points to a female author (424, emphasis added).[21] Again, the reviewer assumes that the audience would accept this conclusion without explanation.

Feminist critic Dale Spender maintains in *Mothers of the Novel* that there is a distinct shift in *Mary Barton*'s reception that shows the negative impact of Gaskell's gender:

When it was believed that *Mary Barton* was written by a man, the *Athenaeum* (1848) was full of praise for the author's grasp of politics

---

[21]I read "internal" to mean evidence from within the novel, as opposed to outside information about the author's identity.

> and the fair and forcible portrayal of the working classes (p. 1050). But when known to be by a woman, the whole tenor of the criticism changed. It is not the political acumen of Elizabeth Gaskell but her ability to promote sympathy which becomes the focal point. Her emotionalism, her lack of objectivity are soon 'discovered' and the broad canvas of class politics is reduced—by the critics—to a 'sweet and fragrant' love story. (164)

I believe that Spender overstates the case: the *Athenaeum*, as I have shown, already puts Gaskell's gender into question, so it doesn't necessarily represent a review of the "male" *Mary Barton*, and the revelation of Gaskell's gender did not prevent the later critics from considering the political views presented in *Mary Barton*.[22] The feminization of *Mary Barton* has a much subtler effect than the simple dismissal of the novel as a love story, but I believe Spender is correct in pointing out that the feminization of the novel led to accusations of emotionalism, lack of objectivity, and, even worse, simple ignorance. Most importantly, the reviews certainly demonstrate that before the publication of *Mary Barton* there was already a set of assumptions in place about social reform discourse—assumptions that kept novels like *Mary Barton* from the highest echelons of literary achievement, even though such novels were often highly regarded in moral, social, and even political, terms. The nineteenth-century reading public came to accept, even to expect, that literary works would address social issues like poverty, poor working and housing conditions, and prostitution, to expect that these works would effect change by influencing the hearts and the feelings of their readers, and to associate this "literature with a purpose" with women writers. These same gendered assumptions, however, affected the reception of Gaskell's work for the worse. Like Dickens and Charlotte Brontë, Gaskell was locked into the gender binaries that

---

[22]Spender's brief analysis is a sidenote to the main argument of *Mothers of the Novel*, which is the resuscitation of seventeenth- and eighteenth-century women novelists. Her description of *Mary Barton*'s reception is intended to support an argument that women writers have often been dismissed through an association with romantic fiction and "love stories."

were the guiding principles of nineteenth-century culture, as exemplified in nineteenth-century literary reception.

Gaskell was to address social issues in at least two other novels: tackling prostitution in *Ruth* (1853) and returning to factory reform in *North and South* (1854). I see *North and South* as a representation of Gaskell's movement away from sentimentalist social reform discourse, but unfortunately, the novel does not replace the sentimentalist model with any other viable pattern for women social reformers, outside of a narrowly defined domestic role. *North and South* depicts an antagonistic relationship between its heroine, Margaret Hale, and her potential suitor, the industrialist John Thornton, against a backdrop of class antagonism and industrial unrest. As Christine Krueger has pointed out, "In the conflict between men and masters, Margaret acts as Gaskell herself had done in *Mary Barton*, as a proper evangelist of reconciliation, defending the poor, but reminding both sides of their moral obligations" (206–7). Although Margaret is able to use this "feminine" power in the novel in order to influence Thornton towards a better, more sympathetic relationship with his workers, the end of the novel presents a disturbing picture of her submission to Thornton and her eventual enclosure within a more narrowly-defined domestic sphere. Margaret's initial understanding of her role as a woman draws on the wider boundaries drawn by Charlotte Elizabeth Tonna's "talent of female influence": being a woman means that Margaret has special access to sympathy and to moral values, which enables her to see Thornton, the workers, and the duties each owe to the other, more perceptively than Thornton can. She combats Thornton's more rigid understanding of gender roles with her insistence on talking about politics, and making suggestions about how Thornton should behave towards his employees.

At the end of the novel, however, Margaret subsides into "delicious silence" (*North and South* 436), and there is no indication that she will continue to influence Thornton with her "womanly instinct" (195). He has, in fact, entirely co-opted Margaret's perspective on his business, leaving her nothing to contribute to their partnership except "deep blushes," "loving eyes," and assertions that she is "not good enough" (435). In the final analysis, *North and South* returns to a depressingly limited picture of what "female influence" can contribute to social debate; this ending could represent, as Krueger has suggested, Gaskell's frustration with her role as woman preacher—a role, I would add, that was mandated by the conventions of sentimentalist social reform discourse.

Eventually, Gaskell abandoned current social issues in her works, and turned to writing pastoral novels, like *Sylvia's Lovers* (1863) and *Wives and Daughters* (1866), which are set in the historical, rural past, much like George Eliot's *Adam Bede* and *Middlemarch*. Edgar Wright theorized in 1965 that this shift in tone and subject matter derived from Gaskell's internal drive for literary excellence, but this conclusion must have come at least in part from Wright's own New Critical conviction that works "written with a sense of obligation towards ideals of moral or public duty" cannot have real literary worth, since he does not provide any evidence from Gaskell's personal writings to support this theory (Wright 146). There is at least as much evidence in what I have presented in this chapter to suggest that the gender politics of sentimentalist discourse and literary reception drove Gaskell away from social problem writing, or at least away from social problem writing that could be easily identified with the conventions of sentimentalist social reform discourse.

Conclusion

This book has important implications, both for Victorian studies and for feminist criticism. First, it investigates a largely unrecognized, but culturally important, tradition; in the process, the project productively expands our understanding of nineteenth-century culture by looking at previously overlooked writers, texts, and literary practices.

I have therefore made a point of dealing extensively with more obscure writers in this book, such as Tonna and Trollope, in order to suggest their significance. I have, however, concentrated on writers who are more or less canonical. This concentration is intended to demonstrate the important cultural influence of sentimentalist social reform fiction on "mainstream" literary figures and in order to show how these authors' use of sentimentalist conventions has affected their literary reception. The analysis of Dickens, for example, shows that the gender expectations set up by the feminization of social reform discourse had a real impact both on Dickens' writing and on the way that writing was received.

The reception history of Gaskell's *Mary Barton* is also significant because it helps to explain how so many sentimentalist women writers could have simply disappeared from literary history. Gaskell's experience, in many ways, exemplifies the problems faced by a woman writer working within the limitations of sentimentalist discourse. While the cultural imperatives of the domestic ideology gave women special access to morality and emotion, granting them a powerful voice in social reform issues, these same cultural imperatives limited women in tone and subject matter because they could only address social issues from this feminized, moralistic perspective. Therefore, while nineteenth-century constructions of femininity which linked women with sentiment and morality gave these women writers a powerful political voice, this voice was inextricably linked to conventions that literary critics would later come to reject.

Another more mainstream woman writer who was deeply influenced and affected by sentimentalist social reform discourse was Elizabeth Barrett Browning. The ups and downs of

Browning's critical reputation clearly demonstrate the fate of sentimentalism in the academic marketplace. Criticism of Browning's sentimentality, however, takes on new meaning when we consider Browning's consistent poetic involvement with social and political issues in works like *Aurora Leigh*, "The Cry of the Children," "A Curse for a Nation," "A Plea for the Ragged Schools of London," and, finally, her poetic works that supported the Italian Revolution.

As Virginia Woolf said, "Fate has not been kind to Mrs. Browning as a writer," and I believe that part of the reason for this fact is that Browning exemplifies the inherent problems and contradictions of a woman writing in the sentimentalist mode. Critics contemporaneous with Browning, such as the *Guardian*'s reviewer of her 1850 Poems, greatly admired her social reform poems for their "romantic feeling and religious spirit" (56). For example, Charles Kingsley responded to 1843's "Cry of the Children," by asking in 1851, "If this lady is not a great poetess, who is?" ("Mr. and Mrs. Browning" 178-82). Reviews of 1860's more forthright and impassioned "A Curse for a Nation"(included in *Poems Before Congress*), however, found the poem distasteful, calling it "oracular raving" (Aytoun 491) with "little sweetness" (qtd. in Donaldson 81). This difference suggests that as far as the contemporary critics were concerned, Barrett Browning's participation in the political arena was only acceptable if it was sentimental. "A Curse for a Nation," even though it comes from "how the heart melts and the tears run down," was considered too harsh and unladylike (Browning 423).

After Browning's death, her critical status became even more vexed. The situation was characterized by one *Macmillan's Magazine* critic in 1888 as follows: "She [Browning] is perhaps too learned for women and too emotional for men," and her audience is thus limited to "intellectual sentimentalists" (Benson 138). In fact, the criticism that Browning's poetry is too sentimental was probably the most damning (and damaging) one leveled at her. In 1916, Arthur Waugh accused Browning of having a "feminine trick of overemphasis and hyperbole" (Waugh 65), and finally, in 1937, American scholar and New Critic, Cornelius Weygandt, dismissed

Browning's "obvious and ill phrased sentimentality" (Weygandt 156).

These examples clearly illustrate that the issue of sentimentality, and especially the issue of sentimentalism (sentimentality in the arena of social reform), is crucial to any reconsideration of Elizabeth Barrett Browning's place in the Victorian period. Recontextualizing her work in the sentimentalist discourse of social reform would interrogate this issue in a new way because it shows how Browning entered into public/political discourse with her "acceptable" use of the sentimental, the same quality that contributed to her later exclusion from the canon.

Finally, in order to conclude this book I want to return to the issue with which I ended its first chapter: the vexed issue of how we should deal with sentimentalism in feminist criticism.

When I began to do my research on Charlotte Elizabeth Tonna, I had to obtain many of her works through Interlibrary Loan. When I went to the library to ask for my copy of *The Wrongs of Woman*, the young woman at the desk started, guiltily, and then said, "Oh, I was hoping that you wouldn't come for another couple of days—I've been reading that one." Since, like most scholars, I am amazed when "normal" people from the outside world take an interest in what I'm researching, I wasn't quite prepared for her next question. She said, "I don't understand this writer. I started reading thinking that this was a feminist book because of the title, but I'm really confused because of all this stuff that says women are sinful and not equal to men. Was this writer a feminist or not?"

Her question points to the crux of the issue. Are writers like Tonna, who constantly deny that they seek equality for women, valid subjects for feminist study? In her introduction to *The Wrongs of Woman*, Tonna states that "if we undertake to discuss the wrongs of women, we may be expected to set out by plainly defining what are the rights of women. This is soon done. We repudiate all pretensions to equality with man save on the ground specified by the Apostle [Paul], that 'In Christ Jesus, there is neither male nor female'" (3). Tonna also concedes Eve's responsibility for the Fall, but then, however, she goes on to hint that female faults are caused by the "greater feebleness and dependency" of women, which, in turn, are caused by social oppression (10). The whole book, from that point, goes on to address the wrongs of women, progressing from the factory system that Tonna blames for the breakup of the family, to the great evil of child labor in "The Little Pin-Headers," and the hardship of seamstresses in "The Lace-Runners." So, in the sense that she responds to the social oppression of women, Tonna is a feminist in the tradition of Mary Wollstonecraft. And in that sense, it is no surprise that her book's title is the same as the subtitle of Mary Wollstonecraft's unfinished novel *Maria; or, the Wrongs of Woman*.

Tonna's refusal to embrace women's suffrage and her conformity to traditional social and religious conventions make her inconsistent, however, with twentieth-century feminist ideals. It is in response to these inconsistencies that feminists like Elaine Showalter and Ann Douglas have failed to embrace sentimentalist authors as part of the feminist literary tradition. As I contended in the first chapter, I believe that part of this failure comes from the influence of formalist literary criticism, but part of it also comes from a liberal/rationalist feminist tradition that is inextricably linked to the myth of the "extraordinary" woman. This tradition rejects women writers who conformed with the social and religious values that are seen as patriarchal and instead celebrates those who are seen as in rebellion against these values. Conversely, I am not saying that we should turn this formula inside out and celebrate "ordinary" women writers at the expense of "extraordinary" women writers. Instead, I do not believe that it is an either/or situation.

What we need to realize is that the seeming conservatism of sentimentalist discourse may have actually contributed to, not limited, the eventual enfranchisement of women. For one thing, sentimentalist discourse offered a medium through which women could participate in the political arena and still conform to nineteenth-century definitions of femininity. This in itself makes it a phenomenon worthy of feminist study. Secondly, some historians have theorized that women's increasing involvement in worldly affairs through their growing dominance of philanthropic institutions gradually led to their involvement explicitly political movements, such as women's suffrage. This is a thesis that has been advanced by historian F.M. Prochaska:

> The charitable experience of women was a lever which they [women] used to open the doors closed to them in other spheres. . . . It should not come as a surprise that in 1866 women trained in charitable societies were prominent among those who petitioned the House of Commons praying for the enfranchisement of their sex. (226-227)

Prochaska's conclusions are supported by a later text as well, a collection of papers on "the philanthropic work of women" arranged and edited by Angela Burdett-Coutts.[1]

The very scope and nature of this collection, which incorporates reports from women from many parts of Britain and engaged in almost every kind of charitable enterprise, emphasize that it celebrates "organized philanthropic effort on a broad scale"—in other words, philanthropy in the same businesslike, officious, and organized form that was so deplored by Dickens in *Bleak House*. The reports themselves incorporate "masculine" statistics, charts, and tables, and were obviously solicited and produced in a formal and systematic manner. One cannot help but be impressed by the extent of these women's activities. However, Coutts also stresses the personal and emotional side of women's charity:

> To this hour, and all over the country, there are a thousand little centres of benevolence which find no record here, nor indeed anywhere else, if not in the book of the Recording Angel. The fortunes of the squirearchy have fallen very much, but the mansion and manor-house have not given up the old kindly duties, while in every town, and in every parish of the

---

[1]This collection of papers was submitted to Princess Christian of Schleswig-Holstein who, according to Coutt's introduction, had apparently requested a report on Englishwomen's charitable work to be displayed at the Chicago Exhibition. The purpose of the report was to bring these philanthropic activities "to the knowledge of their [Englishwomen's] kinsfolk across the seas . . . and join . . . all nations of the world in a common bond of sympathy with Women's Philanthropic Work" (*Woman's Mission* vii). This collection was then published in 1893, both New York and London.

> greater towns, you may find little coteries of good women who work together for the poor and helpless about them without a thought of dignifying their quiet labours by carrying them on under the name of Society or Association. (xvii)

This paradox, the contrast between Coutts' presentation of the active and methodical *business* of charity and her emphasis on the small, the spontaneous, and the unrecognized *duties* of female charity, clearly derives from Coutts' reliance on sentimentalist cultural attitudes. The contradiction even shows up on the title page, where the book's ambitious title, *Woman's Mission: a Series of Congress Papers on the Philanthropic Work of Women by Eminent Writers*, is followed by an epigraph from Chaucer, "So womanlie, so benigne, and so meeke." The book's purpose is to celebrate woman's mission and woman's work (and these title words do not refer to "traditional" women's work, such as cleaning, cooking, or child-rearing); yet, this work and this mission both rely on sentimentalist assumptions about the "natural" sympathy and kindness of women:

> It is fitting that the close of the nineteenth century should focus and illustrate in a definite form the share which women have taken it its development, of which, in my humble judgment, the truest and noblest, because the most natural, part, is to be found in philanthropic work. (*Woman's Mission* ix).

Since, as *Woman's Mission* shows, women's involvement in philanthropy was closely connected to a sentimentalist cultural discourse that taught women (as well as men) to respond benevolently to social problems, sentimentalist texts, such as those by Tonna, Trollope, and others, are also an important part of the evolution in women's political consciousness.

As cultural theorist Michel Foucault has argued, power is essentially diffuse in nature and can be exerted in more ways than just one:

> Power comes from below; that is, there is no binary and all-encompassing opposition between rulers and ruled at the root of power relations, and serving as a general matrix--no such duality extending from the top down and reacting on more and more limited groups to the very depths of the social body. One must suppose rather that the manifold productions of

force that take shape and come into play in the machinery of production, in families, limited groups and institutions, are the basis for wide-ranging effects of cleavage that run through the social body as a whole. (94)

Since sentimentalist texts had a powerful social influence, they can certainly be defined as a "production of force" under this definition. In order to truly account for the full range of women's achievements in the nineteenth-century, we need to recognize all of these exertions of female power, not just confine ourselves to those of a few "extraordinary" women, and/or ignore texts (or parts of texts) because they make use of forces that we disagree with. In *Mothers of the Novel* (1986), for instance, Dale Spender presented the novelist Mary Brunton (1778–1818) for special mention as a "first rate and forgotten woman writer" (325). Spender, however, qualifies this recommendation with this disclaimer:

> I have a real problem with her [Brunton's] overt use of Christian dogma as the explanation and justification of moral development. This discomfort which I feel with her explicit religious sentiments could be the result of their 'inappropriateness' in a contemporary (and post-Freudian) context: more likely, however, is that it is the result of my personal prejudice. . . . [I]was able to employ the tried and true literary strategy of 'skipping' the pages on which they [the passages of pious prose] occurred. (325)

Another example of the ill-effects of this blind spot in some feminist criticism is the status of the nineteenth-century French novelist George Sand. Although Sand's importance is obvious, feminism has had difficulty coming to terms with some aspects of her work. As Erdmute Wenzel White points out in her 1988 article "George Sand: Muse or Anti-Muse," Sand often "emerges as culturally conservative and conformist, at least in some major aspects of her life and work" (White 146). In 1837, for example, George Sand wrote her *Lettres à Marcie* which, addressed to an imaginary unwed girl of 25, were a comprehensive exposition of Sand's views on the woman question. In these letters, which would be anathema to any feminist today, Sand preaches a romantic ideal that denies the material equality of women, while it exalts their moral and spiritual superiority. She believes that "women are not suited to the posts which the laws have heretofore denied them,", and upholds that great nineteenth-century model of woman as mother: "all calm, kindness, serenity, and angelic sentiment" (qtd. in Cate 418–419). Sand here seems to create two entirely different spheres of human action: a male, and a female—a formula that, like sentimentalism, draws on the gender binaries of the nineteenth-century domestic ideology.

It is Sand's apparent conservatism, her stated belief in an "repressive" ethic which seems to reinforce the powerlessness of women, that has made it so difficult for feminist scholars to come to terms with her. Did this groundbreaking woman novelist, seemingly so radical and liberated in her own lifestyle, consistently adhere to, and even proselytize, this patriarchal nineteenth-century ideal that made it necessary for women to suffer and selflessly sacrifice their own happiness in order to maintain their "redemptive" moral superiority over men?

It is questions like these that lead feminist scholars to exclude certain kinds of texts. When we catch ourselves deciding not to teach or study a text for such reasons, however, our criticism becomes suspect. In order to understand our history as women, we need to historicize our assessments of women's writing. In *Beyond a Feminist Aesthetic*, Rita Felski suggests a similar historical approach:

> [T]he political meanings of women's writing cannot be theorized in an a priori fashion, by appealing to an inherent relationship between gender and a specific linguistic or literary form, but can be addressed only by relating the diverse forms of women's writing to the cultural and ideological processes shaping the effects and potential limits of literary production at historically specific contexts. (48)

If, by doing so, we can add to our appreciation of women writers' impressive achievements, that process can only enhance our feminism, not detract from it.

Bibliography

Ackroyd, Peter. *Dickens*. New York: HarperCollins, 1990.
Alexander, Lynn M. and Sharon A. Winn, eds. *The Slaughter-House of Mammon: An Anthology of Victorian Social Protest Literature*. West Cornwall, CT: Locust Hill Press, 1992.
Altick, Richard. *The English Common Reader: A Social History of the Mass Reading Public, 1800–1900*. Chicago: University of Chicago Press, 1957.
———. *The Presence of the Present: Topics of the Day in the Victorian Novel*.Columbus: Ohio State University Press, 1991.
Armstrong, Isobel. "Gush of the Feminine: How Can We Read Women's Poetry of the Romantic Period?" *Romantic Women Writers: Voices and Countervoices*. Eds. Paula R. Feldman and Theresa M. Kelley. Hanover: University Press of New England, 1995.
Armstrong, Nancy. *Desire and Domestic Fiction*. New York: Oxford University Press, 1987.
Ashton, Rosemary. *George Eliot: A Life*. London: Allen Lane, The Penguin Press, 1996.
Aytoun, William Edmounstone. "Poetic Aberrations." *Blackwood's Edinburgh Magazine* 87 (1860): 490–4.
Barker-Benfield, G.J. *The Culture of Sensibility: Sex and Society in Eighteenth-Century Britain*. Chicago: The University of Chicago Press, 1992.
Baym, Nina. *Woman's Fiction: A Guide to Novels by and about Women in America, 1820–1870*. Ithica: Cornell University Press, 1978.
Benson, Arthur C. "Mrs. Browning." *Macmillan's Magazine* 59 (1888): 138-45.
Bodenheimer, Rosemarie. *The Politics of Story in Victorian Social Fiction*. Ithica: Cornell University Press, 1988.
The Book of Hymns: Official Hymnal of the United Methodist Church. Nashville: The United Methodist Publishing House, 1966.
Brissenden, R.F. *Virtue in Distress: Studies in the Novel of Sentiment from Richardson to Sade*. New York: Macmillan, 1974.
Brontë, Charlotte. *Shirley*. London: Oxford University Press, 1981.
Burke, Kenneth. *Counter-Statement*. Berkeley: University of California Press, 1968.

———. *A Rhetoric of Motives*. Berkeley: University of California Press, 1969.
Cate, Curtis. *George Sand*. Boston: Houghton Mifflin, 1975.
Cazamian, Louis. *The Social Novel in England: 1830–1850*. trans. Martin Fido. Boston: Routledge and Kegan Paul, 1973.
Clark, Suzanne. *Sentimental Modernism*. Bloomington: Indiana University Press, 1991.
Cockburn, Lord. *Life of Lord Jeffrey With a Selection from His Correspondence*. Vols. I–II. Edinburgh, 1852.
Codell, Julie F. "Sentiment, the Highest Attribute of Art: the Socio-Poetics of Feeling." *Dickens Studies Annual* 21 (1992): 233–252.
Colby, Robert. *Fiction With a Purpose: Major and Minor Nineteenth-Century Novels*. Bloomington: Indiana University Press, 1967.
Collins, Philip, ed. *Dickens: the Critical Heritage*. New York: Barnes and Noble, Inc., 1971.
———, ed. *Dickens: Interviews and Recollections*. 2 vols. London: The Macmillan Press, 1981.
Craik, Dinah Mulock. *A Woman's Thoughts About Women*. New York: Rudd and Carleton, 1858.
———. *John Halifax, Gentleman*. London: Hurst and Blackett, 1856.
———."To Novelists—and a Novelist." *MacMillan's* 3 (1861): 441–448.
Croly, George. "Remarks on Shelley's *Adonais*." *Blackwood's Edinburgh Magazine* 10 (Dec. 1821), 696–700.
Cross, Wilbur. *The Development of the English Novel*. London: Macmillan & Co., 1899.
Cuddon, J. A. *The Penguin Dictionary of Literary Terms and Literary Theory, Third Edition*. London: Penguin Books, 1992.
Curran, Stuart. "The I Altered." *Romanticism and Feminism*. ed. Anne K. Mellor. Bloomington: Indiana University Press, 1988.
Cvetkovich, Ann. *Mixed Feelings: Feminism, Mass Culture, and Victorian Sensationalism*. New Brunswick: Rutgers University Press, 1992.
Dalziel, Margaret. *Popular Fiction 100 Years Ago*. London: Cohen and West, 1957.
David, Deirdre. *Fictions of Resolution in Three Victorian Novels: North and South, Our Mutual Friend, and Daniel Deronda*. New York: Columbia University Press, 1981.
———. *Intellectual Women and Victorian Patriarchy: Harriet Martineau, Elizabeth Barrett Browning, George Eliot*. London: The Macmillan Press, 1987.

Davidoff, Leonore and Catherine Hall. *Family Fortunes: Men and Women of the English Middle Class, 1780–1850*. Chicago: University of Chicago Press, 1987.
Dickens, Charles. *Bleak House*. Ed. Norman Page. London: Penguin, 1971.
———. *The Christmas Books, vol. I*. Ed. Michael Slater. London: Penguin, 1971.
———. *Dombey and Son*. Ed. Peter Fairclough. London: Penguin, 1970.
———. *Hard Times*. Eds. George Ford and Sylvere Monod. New York: W.W. Norton and Co., 1990.
———. *Letters of Charles Dickens*. vols. 1–10. eds. Madeleine House and Graham Storey, et al. Oxford: Clarendon Press, 1965–1988.
———. *The Life and Adventures of Nicholas Nickleby*. 2 vols. ed. Michael Slater. Philadelphia: The University of Pennsylvania Press, 1982.
———. *Little Dorrit*. Ed. Harvey Peter Sucksmith. New York: Oxford University Press, 1982.
———. *Oliver Twist*. Ed. Peter Fairclough. London: Penguin, 1966.
———. "On Strike." *Household Words* 11 February, 1854, 553–559.
———. *Our Mutual Friend*. Ed. Stephen Gill. London: Penguin, 1971.
———. *The Personal History of David Copperfield*. New York, n.d.
———. *Speeches*. ed. K.J. Fielding. Oxford: Clarendon Press, 1960.
Dickens, Charles and Henry Morley. "Our Wicked Mis-Statements." *Household Words* 13 (19 January, 1856): 13–19.
Disraeli, Benjamin. *Sybil*. London: Longmans and Co., 1920.
Donaldson, Sandra. *Elizabeth Barrett Browning: An Annotated Bibliography of the Commentary and Criticism, 1826–1990*. New York: G. K. Hall and Co., 1993.
Douglas, Ann. *The Feminization of American Culture*. New York: Alfred A. Knopf, Inc., 1977.
Dyos, H.J. *Exploring the Urban Past*. eds. David Cannadine and David Reeder. New York: Cambridge University Press, 1982.
Eagleton, Mary. *Feminist Literary Theory*. Oxford: Basil Blackwell, 1988.
Eagleton, Terry. *Literary Theory*. Minneapolis: University of Minnesota Press, 1983.

Edgar, Pelham. *The Art of the Novel from 1700 to the Present Time.* New York: MacMillan, 1934.

Eliot, George. *Essays of George Eliot.* Ed. Thomas Pinney. New York: Columbia University Press, 1963.

Eliot, T.S. *Selected Essays (New Edition).* New York: Harcourt Brace, Jovanovich, 1950.

Ellis, Markman. *The Politics of Sensibility: Race, Gender, and Commerce in the Sentimental Novel.* Cambridge: Cambridge University Press, 1996.

Ellis, William and Mary Turner Ellis. Rev. of *Mary Barton*, by Elizabeth Gaskell. *The Westminster and Foreign Quarterly Review.* April, 1849: 48–63.

Ellman, Richard. *Oscar Wilde.* New York: Alfred A. Knopf, 1988.

Engels, Frederick. *The Condition of the Working Class in England.* trans. and eds. W.O. Henderson and W.H. Chaloner. Oxford: Basil Blackwell, 1958.

Erämetsä, Erik. *A Study of the Word 'Sentimental' and Other Linguistic Characteristics of Eighteenth-Century Sentimentalism in England.* Helsinki, 1951.

Feldman, Paula R. and Theresa M. Kelley, eds. *Romantic Women Writers: Voices and Countervoices.* Hanover: University Press of New England, 1995.

Felski, Rita. *Beyond Feminist Aesthetics.* Cambridge: Harvard University Press, 1989.

Ferris, Ina. "From Trope to Code: the Novel and the Rhetoric of Gender in Nineteenth-century Critical Discourse." *Rewriting the Victorians.* Ed. Linda Shires. New York: Routledge, 1992.

Fielding, K.J. and Anne Smith. "*Hard Times* and the Factory Controversy: Dickens and Harriet Martineau." *Dickens Centennial Essays.* Eds. Blake Nevius and Ada Nisbet. Berkeley: University of California Press, 1971.

Fielding, K.J. "Benthamite Utilitarianism and Oliver Twist: A Novel of Ideas." *Dickens Quarterly* 4 (1987): 49–65.

Ford, George H. *Dickens and His Readers: Aspects of Novel Criticism Since 1836.* Princeton: Princeton University Press, 1955.

Ford, Richard. Rev. of *Oliver Twist*, by Charles Dickens. *Quarterly Review* 64 (1839): 83–102.

Foucault, Michel. *The History of Sexuality, Vol. I.* Trans. Robert Hurley. New York: Vintage Books, 1990.

Fryckedstedt, Monica. "Charlotte Elizabeth Tonna and the *Christian Lady's Magazine.*" *Victorian Periodicals Review* 14 (1981): 43–51.

———."The Early Industrial Novel: *Mary Barton* and its Predecessors." *Bulletin of the John Rylands University of Manchester* 63 (1980): 11–30.

———. *Elizabeth Gaskell's Mary Barton and Ruth: A Challenge to Christian England.* Doctoral Thesis, Uppsala University, 1982. Studia Anglistica Upsaliensia 43.

Gallagher, Catherine. *The Industrial Reformation of English Fiction.* Chicago: The University of Chicago Press, 1985.

Gaskell, Elizabeth. *The Letters of Mrs. Gaskell.* Eds. J.A.V. Chapple and Arthur Pollard. Manchester: Manchester University Press, 1966.

———. *The Life of Charlotte Brontë.* Ed. Alan Shelston. London: Penguin, 1985.

———. *Mary Barton.* Ed. Edgar Wright. New York; Oxford University Press, 1987.

———. *North and South.* Ed. Angus Easson. New York: Oxford University Press, 1992.

———. *Ruth.* Ed. Alan Shelston. New York: Oxford University Press, 1985.

Gérin, Winifred. *Elizabeth Gaskell: A Biography.* Oxford: Clarendon Press, 1976.

Gilbert, Sandra and Susan Gubar. *The Madwoman in the Attic: The Woman Writer and the Nineteenth-Century Literary Imagination.* New Haven: Yale University Press, 1979.

Gilmour, Robin. *The Novel in the Victorian Age.* London: Edward Arnold, Ltd., 1986.

Goode, John. "Mrs. Gaskell and Brotherhood." *Tradition and Tolerance in Nineteenth-Century Fiction.* Eds. David Howard, John Lucas, and John Goode. New York: Barnes and Noble, 1967.

Greg, W.R. "The False Morality of Lady Novelists." *The National Review* 8 (1859): 144–169.

———. Rev. of *Mary Barton,* by Elizabeth Gaskell. *The Edinburgh Review.* January–April, 1849: 207–224.

Gross, John. *The Rise and Fall of the Man of Letters: A Study of the Idiosyncratic and the Humane in Modern Literature.* New York: Macmillan, 1969.

Hadley, Elaine. *Melodramatic Tactics: Theatricalized Dissent in the English Marketplace, 1800-1885.* Stanford: Stanford University Press, 1995.

Hardy, Barbara. *The Moral Art of Dickens.* New York: Oxford University Press, 1975.

Hazlitt, William. *The Complete Works of William Hazlitt: Centenary Edition.* Ed. P.P. Howe. Vol. 4. London: J.M. Dent and Sons, 1930.

Heineman, Helen. *Mrs. Trollope: the Triumphant Feminine in the Nineteenth Century.* Athens: Ohio University Press, 1979.

Himmelfarb, Gertrude. *The Idea of Poverty: England in the Early Industrial Age.* New York: Knopf, 1984.

Hutton, Richard Holt. "Novels by the Authoress of John Halifax." *North British Review.* 29 (1858): 466–481.

Jaffe, Audrey. "Spectacular Sympathy: Visuality and Ideology in Dickens' *A Christmas Carol.*" *PMLA* 109 (1994): 254–265.

James, Louis. *Fiction for the Working Man.* London: Oxford University Press, 1963.

Jay, Elizabeth. *The Religion of the Heart: Anglican Evangelicalism and the Nineteenth-Century Novel.* Oxford: Clarendon Press, 1979.

Johnson, Claudia. *Equivocal Beings: Politics, Gender, and Sentimentality in the 1790's.* Chicago: The University of Chicago Press, 1995.

Johnson, Edgar. *Charles Dickens: His Tragedy and Triumph.* 2 vols. New York: Simon and Schuster, 1952.

Kanner, Barbara and Ivanka Kovacevic. "Blue Book into Novel: the Forgotten Industrial Fiction of Charlotte Elizabeth Tonna." *Nineteenth Century Fiction* 25 (1970): 152–173.

Kaplan, Fred. *Sacred Tears: Sentimentality in Victorian Literature.* Princeton: Princeton University Press, 1987.

Kestner, Joseph. "Charlotte Elizabeth Tonna's *The Wrongs of Woman*: Female Industrial Protest." *Tulsa Studies in Women's Literature* 2 (1983): 193–214.

———. *Protest and Reform: The British Social Narrative By Women, 1827–1867.* Madison: The University of Wisconsin Press, 1985.

Kingsley, Charles. Rev. of *Mary Barton*, by Elizabeth Gaskell. *Fraser's Town and Country Magazine.* April, 1849: 429–432.

———. Rev. of Poems (1850), by Elizabeth Barrett Browning. *Fraser's Town and Country Magazine.* February 1851: 178–82.

Kovacevic, Ivanka. *Fact into Fiction*. Chatham: Leicester University Press, 1975.

Krueger, Christine. *The Reader's Repentance: Women Preachers, Women Writers, and Nineteenth-Century Social Discourse*. Chicago: the University of Chicago Press, 1992.

"The Lady Novelists of Great Britain."*Gentleman's Magazine* 40 (1853): 18–25.

Larson, Janet. *Dickens and The Broken Scripture*. Athens: The University of Georgia Press, 1985.

Leavis, F.R. and Q.D. *Dickens the Novelist*. New York: Pantheon Books, 1970.

Lewes, George Henry. Rev. of *Shirley*, by Charlotte Bronte. *Edinburgh Review*. January, 1850: 153–173.

———. "The Lady Novelists." *Westminster Review* 58 (1852): 129–141.

Lewis, Clarendon and Charles Short. *A Latin Dictionary*. Oxford: Clarendon Press, 1962 ed.

Lockhart, John Gibson. "The Cockney School of Poetry." *Blackwood's Edinburgh Magazine* 3 (August, 1818): 519–524.

"Loose Thoughts." *Fraser's Town and Country Magazine*. 18 (1838), 500.

"The Manufacturing Poor: The Means of Elevating Their Moral Condition—Education." *Fraser's Town and Country Magazine*. 39 (1849): 127–143.

Marcus, Steven. *Dickens from Pickwick to Dombey*. New York: W.W. Norton and Co., 1965.

Martineau, Harriet. *Autobiography*. 2 vols. ed. Maria Weston Chapman. Boston: Houghton and Mifflin and Co., 1877.

———. *The Factory Controversy: A Warning Against Meddling Legislation*. Manchester, 1855.

———. *Selected Letters*. ed. Valerie Sanders. Oxford: Clarendon Press, 1990.

Mayhew, Henry. *London Labour and the London Poor*. Ed. Victor Neuberg. London: Penguin, 1985.

McGuirk, Carol. *Robert Burns and the Sentimental Era*. Athens: The University of Georgia Press, 1985.

Mellor, Anne K. *Romanticism and Gender*. New York: Routledge, Chapman, and Hall, 1993.

Meredith, George. *An Essay on Comedy and the Uses of the Comic Spirit*. Ed. Lane Cooper. Ithica: Cornell University Press, 1918.

———. *Miscellaneous Prose*. London: Constable and Co., 1910.

Mill, John Stuart. *The Subjection of Women*. New York: Appleton and Company, 1869.

Miller, J. Hillis. Introduction. *Bleak House*. By Charles Dickens. New York: Penguin, 1971.

More, Hannah. *Cheap Repository Tracts*. vols. 1–8. New York: American Tract Society, n.d.

The New Oxford Annotated Bible With the Apocrypha. New York: Oxford University Press, 1977.

Newton, Judith. "Engendering History for the Middle Class: Sex and Political Economy in the *Edinburgh Review*." *Rewriting the Victorians*. Ed. Linda Shires. New York: Routledge, 1992.

Norton, Caroline. "A Voice from the Factories." *The Dream and Other Poems*. Boston: Munro and Francis, 1845.

"Novels With a Purpose." *Westminster Review* 26 (1864): 24–49.

Oliphant, Margaret. "Charles Dickens." *Blackwood's Edinburgh Magazine*. 77 (1855): 451-466.

Oxford English Dictionary. Vol. IX. Oxford: Clarendon Press, 1933.

Paroissien, David. *A Companion to Oliver Twist*. Edinburgh: Edinburgh University Press, 1992.

———. "*Oliver Twist* and the Contours of Early Victorian England." *The Victorian Newsletter* Spring, 1993: 14–17.

Pater, Walter. *Appreciations with an Essay on Style*. London: Macmillan and Co., 1918.

Poovey, Mary. *The Proper Lady and the Woman Writer*. Chicago: The University of Chicago Press, 1984.

Pope, Norris. *Dickens and Charity*. New York: Columbia University Press, 1978.

Prochaska, F.M. *Women and Philanthropy in Nineteenth-Century England*. Oxford: Clarendon Press, 1980.

Ransom, Arthur Crowe. *The New Criticism*. Norfolk, Conneticut: New Directions, 1941.

Rev. of *Mary Barton*, by Elizabeth Gaskell. *The Athenaeum* 1848: 1050–51.

Rev. of *Mary Barton*, by Elizabeth Gaskell. *The British Quarterly Review* February–May, 1849: 117–136.

Rev. of *Mary Barton*, by Elizabeth Gaskell. *North British Review* 15 May–August 1851: 419–427.

Richards, I.A. *Practical Criticism*. New York: Harcourt Brace, 1929.

Richardson, Alan. "Romanticism and the Colonization of the Feminine." *Romanticism and Feminism*. ed. Anne Mellor. Bloomington: Indiana University Press, 1988.

Ross, Marlon B. *The Contours of Masculine Desire: Romanticism and the Rise of Women's Poetry*. New York: Oxford University Press, 1989.
Rousseau, Jean-Jacques. *Emile*. Ed. Allan Bloom. New York: Basic Books, 1979.
Schor, Hilary. "Elizabeth Gaskell: A Critical History and a Critical Revision." *Dickens Studies Annual* 19 (1990): 345–369.
———. *Scheherezade in the Marketplace*. New York: Oxford University Press, 1992.
Shelley, Percy. *Shelley's Poetry and Prose*. Eds. Donald H. Reiman and Sharon Powers. New York: WW. Norton and Co., 1977.
Sheppard, Francis. *London 1808–1870: the Infernal Wen*. Berkeley: The University of California Press, 1971.
Showalter, Elaine. "Dinah Mulock Craik and the Tactics of Sentiment." *Feminist Studies* 2 (1975), 152–73
———. *A Literature of Their Own: British Women Novelists from Bronte to Lessing*. Princeton: Princeton University Press, 1977.
Slater, Michael. "The Composition and Monthly Publication of Nicholas Nickleby." *The Life and Adventures of Nicholas Nickleby*. ed. Michael Slater. Philadelphia: The University of Pennsylvania Press, 1982.
Smith, Adam. *The Theory of Moral Sentiments*. Ed. E.G. West. Indianapolis: Liberty Classics, 1976.
Smith, Sheila. *The Other Nation*. Oxford: Clarendon Press, 1980.
Spender, Dale. *Mothers of the Novel: One Hundred Good Women Writers Before Jane Austen*. New York: Pandora Press, 1986.
Stedman-Jones, Gareth. *Outcast London*. Oxford: Clarendon Press, 1971.
Stephen, Fitzjames. "Mr. Dickens as a Politician." *Saturday Review of Politics, Literature, Science, and Art*. Vol. 3. (1857): 8–9.
Stoneman, Patsy. *Elizabeth Gaskell*. Bloomington: Indiana University Press, 1987.
Stowe, Harriet Beecher. *Uncle Tom's Cabin*. New York: W.W. Norton and Co., 1994.
———. Introduction. *The Works of Charlotte Elizabeth*. By Charlotte Elizabeth Tonna. New York: M.W. Dodd, 1844.
Tillotson, Kathleen. *Novels of the Eighteen-Forties*. London: Oxford University Press, 1956.
Thompson, E.P. *The Making of the English Working Class*. New York: Vintage Books, 1966.
———. "The Moral Economy of the English Crowd in the Eighteenth Century." *Past and Present* 50 (1971), 76–136.

Tobin, Beth. *Superintending the Poor*. New Haven: Yale University Press, 1993.
Todd, Janet. *Feminist Literary History: A Defence*. Cambridge: Polity Press, 1988.
———. *Sensibility: An Introduction*. London: Methuen, 1986.
Tompkins, Jane. *Sensational Designs*. New York: Oxford University Press, 1985.
Tonna, Charlotte Elizabeth. *Helen Fleetwood*. London: R.B. Seeley, 1848.
———. *Perils of the Nation*. London: Seeley, Burnside, and Seeley, 1843.
———. *Personal Recollections*. London: R.B. Seeley, 1841.
———. "Politics." *Christian Lady's Magazine* March, 1834.
———. *The System*. London: F. Westley and A.H. Davis, 1827.
———. *The Works of Charlotte Elizabeth*. New York: M.W. Dodd, 1844.
———. *The Wrongs of Woman*. New York: M.W. Dodd, 1845.
Trollope, Anthony. *Barchester Towers and The Warden*. New York: Random House, 1936.
Trollope, Frances. *The Life and Adventures of Michael Armstrong, Factory Boy*. London: H. Colburn, 1840.
Tuchman, Gaye. *Edging Women Out: Victorian Novelists, Publishers, and Social Change*. (1989)
Tyrrell, Alex. "'Woman's Mission' and Pressure Group Politics in Britain (1825–1860)." *Bulletin of the John Rylands University Library of Manchester* 63 (Autumn 1980):194–230.
Uglow, Jenny. *Elizabeth Gaskell: A Habit of Stories*. Boston: Faber and Faber, 1993.
Walkowitz, Judith. *City of Dreadful Delight*. London: Virago Press, 1992.
Warhol, Robyn. *Gendered Interventions: Narrative Discourse in the Victorian Novel*. New Brunswick: Rutgers University Press, 1989.
Waugh, Arthur. "The Poetry of Emotion." *Reticence in Literature and Other Papers*. London: J. G. Wilson, 1916.
Webb, R.K. *Harriet Martineau: A Radical Victorian*. New York: Columbia University Press, 1960.
Welsh, Alexander. *The City of Dickens*. Cambridge: Harvard University Press, 1971.
Weygandt, Cornelius. "Elizabeth Barrett Browning." *The Time of Tennyson: English Victorian Poetry as it Affected America*. New York: Appleton Century Co., 1937.

White, Erdmute Wenzel. "George Sand: Muse or Anti-Muse?" *Women in French Literature*. ed. Michel Guggenheim. Stanford French and Italian Studies, 1988. 145-156.
Wilde, Oscar. *Complete Works of Oscar Wilde*. London: Collins, 1966.
Williams, Raymond. *The Country and the City*. New York: Oxford University Press, 1973.
———. *Culture and Society: 1790–1950*. New York: Harper and Row, 1958.
———. Introduction. *Dombey and Son*. By Charles Dickens. London: Penguin, 1970.
———. *Marxism and Literature*. Oxford: Oxford University Press, 1977.
Wilson, Angus. Introduction. *Oliver Twist*. By Charles Dickens. London: Penguin, 1966.
Wohl, Anthony. *The Eternal Slum: Housing and Social Policy in Victorian London*. Montreal: McGill-Queen's University Press, 1977.
Wollstonecraft, Mary. *Vindication of the Rights of Woman*. Ed. Miriam Brody. London: Penguin, 1983.
Woman's Mission: a Series of Congress Papers on the Philanthropic Work of Women by Eminent Writers. Ed. Angela Burdett-Coutts. New York: Charles Scribner's Sons, 1893.
Woolf, Virginia. *A Room of One's Own*. New York: Harcourt Brace Jovanovich, 1929.
———. "Professions for Women." *Feminist Literary Theory*. Ed. Mary Eagleton. Oxford: Basil Blackwell, 1986.
Wright, Edgar. *Mrs. Gaskell: the Basis for Reassessment*. London: Oxford University Press, 1965.
Yeazell, Ruth. "Why Political Novels Have Heroines: *Sybil, Mary Barton*, and *Felix Holt*." *Novel: A Forum on Fiction*. 18 (1985): 126-144.

Index

Addison and Steele, 18
Anti-Jacobin, 18
Armstrong, Isobel, 22 n.
Armstrong, Nancy, 6, 19 n., 42, 43, 57–8, 78
Ashley, Lord, 46, 97–8
Athenaeum, 114 n., 129, 130-1
Austen, Jane, 25, 26 n., 39, 45, 111 n.
Barker-Benfield, G. J., 15
Bible, women writers' use of, 1–3, 8, 45, 47, 62–3, 69, 87–8, 117–9, 122, 124–6, 137
Blackwood's Edinburgh Magazine, 20, 21–2
Blanchard, Samuel Laman, 93–94
"Blue Books," the, 98
Bowles, Caroline, 73
Brissenden, R.F., 12, 13
British Quarterly Review, 129–30
Brontë, Charlotte, 25 n., 39, 111 n., 112–3 n.
Brooke, Henry, 15
Browning, Elizabeth Barrett, 56, 112–3, 135–7
Brunton, Mary. 140
Burdett-Coutts, Angela, 104, 139–40
Burke, Kenneth, 29
Canning, George, 18
Carlyle, Jane Welsh, 23–4
Carlyle, Thomas, 79, 129
Cazamian, Louis, 2, 57, 72, 109–10, 118, 119
Chapman and Hall, 83, 114, 127
Clark, Suzanne, 6, 28, 29, 30, 33, 42–3, 44, 82
Cobbett, William, 50

Colburn, Henry, 93–4
Cowper, William, 13 n.
Craik, Dinah Mulock, 25, 35–8, 58 n.
Cross, Wilbur, 81
Curran, Stuart, 22 n.
Cvetkovich, Ann, 57, 65
Dickens, Charles, 1, 2, 7, 21, 23, 28–9, 77–107, 109, 110–11, 112 n., 124, 131, 135, 139; *Barnaby Rudge*, 96; *Bleak House*, 45, 78, 83, 87, 102–6, 139; *A Christmas Carol*, 56, 82 n., 87; *The Chimes*, 52 n., 81 n.; *David Copperfield*, 92; *Dombey and Son*, 78, 81, 87, 105 n.; *Hard Times*, 29, 109; *Little Dorrit*, 1, 87; *Nicholas Nickleby*, 87, 93–5, 96, 98; *The Old Curiosity Shop*, 27, 28–9, 81, 87; *Oliver Twist*, 47, 51–2, 83–92, 93 n., 95, 96, 98; *Our Mutual Friend*, 78, 87
Domestic ideology, the, 23, 24, 32, 34, 36, 47, 58, 60, 61, 65, 68, 78, 92, 99–100, 105, 135, 142
Disraeli, Benjamin, 53, 56, 70
Douglas, Ann, 39, 41–2, 43, 138
Dyos, H.J., 51
Eagleton, Mary, 42
Eagleton, Terry, 29
Edgar, Pelham, 82
Edinburgh Review, 25 n., 130
Eliot, George (Marian Evans), 21, 23, 32, 34-8, 39, 40, 41, 82, 111 n., 133
Eliot, T.S., 30

Engels, Friedrich, 50, 51, 52
Felski, Rita, 142
Fielding, K.J., 88–89 n.
Ford, George, 28–9, 80 n.
Foucault, Michel, 6, 43–4, 140–1
Fraser's Magazine, 97, 128
Fryckedstedt, Monica, 123
Fuller, Margaret, 38, 41
Gallagher, Catherine, 3, 61, 73, 97 n.
Gaskell, Elizabeth, 7, 8, 9, 35, 45, 56, 66, 69, 70, 73, 74, 77, 100, 101, 104, 107, 109–33, 135; *The Life of Charlotte Brontë*, 112–3 n.; *Mary Barton*, 73, 101, 109, 110 n., 111 n., 112 n., 113–32, 135; *North and South*, 45, 73, 132–3; *Ruth*, 132; *Sylvia's Lovers*, 133; *Wives and Daughters*, 133
Gentleman's Magazine, 59–60, 102, 110 n.
Gillray, James, 18
Godwin, William, 19
Greg, W.R., 24, 54, 55, 130
Gross, John, 26
Hazlitt, William, 15
Heineman, Helen, 70, 72, 99, 120
Himmelfarb, Gertrude, 49 n.
Howitt, William, 114
Hume, David, 12
Hutcheson, Francis, 12
Hutton, Richard Holt, 25–6, 37, 58 n., 100
Jacob's Island, 51–2
Jakobson, Roman, 30
Jeffrey, Francis, 81, 82 n.
Jewsbury, Geraldine, 73
Johnson, Edgar, 98

Kanner, Barbara, 73, 74
Kaplan, Fred, 106
Keats, John, 19–21
Kestner, Joseph, 6–8, 54–5, 73–4, 118 n.
Kingsley, Charles, 56, 70, 128
Kovacevic, Ivanka, 73, 74
Krueger, Christine, 6, 8–9, 15 n., 35 n., 47, 55, 73, 77, 79 n., 114, 115, 118, 132, 133
Leavis, F.R. and Q.D., 29, 105 n.
Lewes, George Henry, 24–6, 58 n., 79, 80 n., 113 n.
Locke, John, 11–2
Lockhart, John Gibson, 20
Mackenzie, Henry, 13
Martineau, Harriet, 59, 84–5, 104
Mayne, Fanny, 7, 73
Mellor, Anne, 19–20, 21
Memoir of Robert Blincoe, 98
Meredith, George, 24
Methodism, 4, 13–5
Mill, John Stuart, 33–4, 38
Moers, Ellen, 73
More, Hannah, 3, 8, 12, 45, 48, 60–4, 66–8, 103, 117
New Poor Law, the, 64, 83–4, 85, 96
North British Review, 130
Norton, Caroline, 69, 72
Oliphant, Margaret, 92
Pater, Walter, 26–7, 30
Pope, Norris, 23 n.
Prochaska, F.M., 34 n., 60, 104–5, 139
Ransom, Arthur Crowe, 30
Richards, I.A., 30–31
Richardson, Alan, 19

Richardson, Samuel, 13 n., 16, 19 n., 106
Romanticism, 19–22
Rousseau, Jean-Jacques, 17–18, 32
Rowton, Frederick, 58
Sand, George, 25, 38 n., 60, 111 n., 141–2
Schor, Hilary, 112
Sensibility, 11–5, 16, 18, 32, 42, 106
"Separate spheres" philosophy, see Domestic ideology
Shaftesbury, Earl of, 12, 17
Shelley, Percy, 19, 21–2
Showalter, Elaine, 39–41, 43, 138
Smith, Adam, 12–3
Smith, Charlotte, 13 n.
Smith, Sheila, 52
Spender, Dale, 130–1, 140
Stephen, Fitzjames, 23, 80, 81, 100
Stone, Elizabeth, 73, 112 n.
Stowe, Harriet Beecher, 1 n., 2, 3, 31, 35, 60, 83, 87, 100–1, 104, 124–5, 127, 128
Sympathy, 4, 7, 9, 19, 23, 35, 37, 38, 53, 59, 65, 66, 67, 69, 77, 78, 79, 88, 89, 90, 91, 103, 109, 116, 119, 120. 123, 124, 126, 131, 132, 140
Thompson, E.P., 14, 48–9, 49–50 n., 53, 84 n.
Tobin, Beth, 48 n., 50 n., 66–7, 102, 103–4
Todd, Janet, 12, 14, 17–9, 32
Tompkins, Jane, 2, 3, 6, 28–9, 31, 42–3, 47, 62, 78, 87, 124, 126
Tonna, Charlotte Elizabeth, 1, 3–5, 7, 8, 9, 44, 45, 46, 47, 48, 55, 57, 58, 59, 60–9, 72, 73–4, 78, 79 n., 83, 98, 99 n., 101, 102, 104, 105, 106, 111, 113, 115–23, 129, 132, 135, 137–8, 140; *The Christian Lady's Magazine* (editor), 55, 65; *Helen Fleetwood*, 4, 46, 47, 55, 61, 64–5, 65–6, 68, 69, 72, 74, 98, 113, 118–23; *Perils of the Nation*, 47, 55, 59, 62–3, 64, 66; *Personal Recollections*, 3–4, 61; *The System*, 55, 72; *The Wrongs of Woman*, 55, 62, 68, 69, 73, 116 n., 117, 137–8
Trollope, Frances, 7, 45, 57, 69–72, 73, 74, 83, 92–9, 111, 113, 118 n., 120 n., 135, 140
Uglow, Jenny, 114, 115 n., 129
Utilitarianism, 33, 34, 64, 77, 84, 85, 86, 88, 109
Victoria, Queen, 79
Wesley, Charles, 14
Wesley, John, 13–5
Westminster Review, 24, 54, 56, 57
Wilde, Oscar, 27, 29, 82
Williams, Raymond, 46, 49–50, 75
Wilson, Angus, 86 n.
Wollstonecraft, Mary, 13 n., 32–3, 38, 138
Woolf, Virginia, 32, 38–9, 136
Wright, Edgar, 112, 114 n., 133
Young, Edward, 13 n.

Studies in Nineteenth-Century British Literature

Regina Hewitt, General Editor

Books in this series examine the poetry and prose produced by British writers from the time of the French Revolution to the death of Queen Victoria. Historical events—rather than traditional literary categories or dates—define the scope of the series because they better convey a sense of the social consciousness that animates literary undertakings during this age. While the series includes a wide range of approaches to nineteenth-century British works, its special focus is on studies that relate this literature to its cultural context(s). Manuscripts addressing their subjects' social, political, or historical situations, ideals, influences, or receptions are especially welcome; manuscripts analyzing the implications of classifying this literature as "Romantic" or "Victorian" or of separating it into genres are also encouraged. Authors should write in English, though they may appropriately compare British works with those in other languages.

Authors wishing to have works considered for this series should contact:

Regina Hewitt
c/o Dr. Heidi Burns
Peter Lang Publishing, Inc.
516 N. Charles St., 2nd Floor
Baltimore, MD 21201